UPRIGHT WITH KNICKERS ON

Surviving the Death of a Child

Gina Claye

**and Members of
The Compassionate Friends,
bereaved parents,
siblings and grandparents**

- sharing grief, finding hope -

www.ginaclaye.co.uk

ISBN 978-1-910779-56-9

Typeset by
Oxford eBooks Ltd.
www.oxford-ebooks.com

Oxford eBooks

DEDICATION

In memory of my children
Nikki and Robin
for
bereaved parents, siblings
and grandparents everywhere
and
members of
The Compassionate Friends
who for 50 years
have brought support and comfort to
those who have suffered
the death of a child

- sharing grief, finding hope -

CONTENTS

ACKNOWLEDGEMENTS

Grateful thanks to Mary Hartley, our TCF Librarian, for reading the manuscript, making excellent suggestions, undertaking subsequent research, drawing up a book list, and for her contributions on many subjects. Grateful thanks also to Dr Margaret Brearley, our past Chair of TCF, for proofreading the manuscript and for her valuable contribution on post-traumatic stress disorder. Thanks to The Estate of Harry Corder Greaves for giving permission to include Harry's poem, *Faith*. Finally a huge thank you to all those of you who have contributed to this book, either through our TCF publications in the UK and other countries, or directly to me. A sincere thank you also to those of you I have been unable to contact and to those 'unknown authors' whose words have been too valuable to leave out. Thank-you all for sharing the things that helped you survive the early days, for sharing what helps you to live your lives now, and for sharing the wisdom you have learnt along this path of grief.

FOREWORD

Why the title, 'Upright with Knickers On'?

At a residential weekend for bereaved parents, we were discussing what helps us get up in the morning. After various comments - 'My dog needs letting out into the garden', and 'Some days I can't manage to get out of bed at all' - one person put up her hand and said: 'I say UKO to get myself going'. And what did that mean? 'Upright With Knickers On.'

The phrase has stuck. It seems to be the perfect thing to say when I need to motivate myself to get going. It's the bare necessity of every day - and sometimes all that I can manage. But it also makes me smile, and I need that too.

Just getting out of bed in the morning was a tremendous struggle after my daughter, Nikki, and then my son, Robin, died. I think back now to those very early days, when I was going mad with grief, before I understood that these weird, bizarre feelings would eventually pass, before I discovered that the best medicine was to tell my story and be listened to… before, in fact, I stumbled on The Compassionate Friends.

The Compassionate Friends is a non-religious organisation of bereaved parents, siblings and grandparents offering comfort and support to others similarly bereaved. If you would like to find out more about TCF, go to the website at www.tcf.org.uk.

This book, written with contributions from bereaved parents, siblings and grandparents describes the traumatic grief, anger, guilt, and despair we all experience when our child, sister, brother or grandchild dies. It is important for us to know that we are not alone in feeling that we're going mad or that we want to go to sleep and never wake up. It also helps enormously to realise that these feelings will eventually pass.

At first, it can be tremendously difficult to find a reason to get up and face the day - even to find a reason to go on living. Those of us further on in our grief have written about what helps us get up in the morning and face the day ahead. It describes how, by allowing ourselves to grieve, we eventually learn to live again with hope and meaning in our lives, always carrying our children, siblings or grandchildren with us.

I do hope that reading this book will bring you comfort and some hope, and, most importantly, help you to know that you are not alone.

Gina Claye

MY STORY

It's many years since my two children, Nikki and Robin, died. I have lived through intense grief, utter disbelief, demanding 'Why', not wanting to live, having bizarre and weird thoughts, feeling I'm going mad… but now, many years on, after meeting so many other bereaved parents through The Compassionate Friends and knowing I'm not alone, life has changed for me.

It was a very slow process, but being able to talk about my children and listen to other bereaved parents telling their stories, finally helping and supporting other more newly bereaved parents, grandparents and siblings, I have come to a stage I thought I would never reach: a feeling of purpose to my life, a calm, a realisation that through my love for my children and their love for me, I am living a fulfilled and happy life carrying my children with me.

THIS IS MY STORY
In 1987 my 19 year old daughter, Nikki, died from suicide. I say 'died from suicide' because we say 'died from cancer' and 'died from a heart attack'. You couldn't see Nikki's illness, but it was very much there.

We had taken her to doctors, consultants, and psychiatrists. We had made very sure she knew we loved her just as she was, but it didn't make any difference. In her mind there was only one way to cure the illness, and she took it.

We were utterly devastated. This couldn't happen to us. We were immediately projected onto a different planet. Life was going on around us as normal: people were shopping, walking the dog, stopping for a chat… But we weren't part of it. How on earth were we going to survive?

The day after she died we had a phone call from someone whom I knew but not very well. I can still recall what she said. 'You may not remember me but I wanted you to know that you're not alone. Our son died from suicide too, and I am a teacher and his father is a headmaster. We're normal people and so are you.'

I wasn't alone.

It was utter relief to know that this tragedy which had befallen our family had happened to another normal family. It was a straw to clutch on to. She went on to say that she knew that our life would be full of people coming and going at the moment so she would contact us again in a fortnight's time. I put the phone down still in a blur of unreality. She did contact me and I went over to her house and we told each other our stories over a cup of tea.

I can't begin to describe how comforting and extremely important this phone call was for me immediately after Nikki died, except that if you're a bereaved parent too, you will understand. I was able to share my story with someone who truly understood and I listened to her story and knew I wasn't alone.

***

And then… sixteen years later my 32 year old son, Robin, was taken ill out in Singapore and died from encephalitis. He had been teaching in a primary school. I got a call one night; I had just gone to bed. The call was from the sister of his partner to say that Robin was in hospital and about to have an operation.

I got the next plane out to Singapore and made my way to Raffles hospital. Robin had had the operation but was already in a coma and on life support. He died a couple of days later.

It was all happening again…

FINDING THE COMPASSIONATE FRIENDS

'There are no strangers at TCF meetings - only friends you haven't yet met.'

In those early days after Nikki died, I didn't think I was going to survive, let alone live any kind of life ever again. Mercifully, a friend told us about The Compassionate Friends, an organisation that gives support and comfort to bereaved parents, grandparents and siblings by those similarly bereaved. This resulted in us booking a place on a residential weekend in Manchester for parents bereaved by suicide, at that time called SoS, (Survivors of Suicide).

I almost didn't go. I couldn't face it, but what was the alternative? So I went. I was warmly welcomed, looked after, introduced to other bereaved parents. Some, I began to realise, had survived many years after the death of their child.

'Tell me about Nikki...' I began to talk, the words came and the tears, it didn't matter. They understood. They'd been there. The cup of tea was hot. I wrapped my hands round it and allowed my tense body to relax and sink back into the sofa. I was exhausted, but I had found something I hadn't known existed but very much needed.

On the Sunday morning in the lounge I sat with a very newly bereaved mum. Her son had died by putting a hosepipe in the car. She was having nightmares imagining the act which she thought must have been painful and how he must have suffered physically by doing that.

I was able to tell her that my daughter had died the same way, but not at the first attempt. I was able to reassure this mum that I knew from our daughter's experience that he would not have suffered physical pain.

It was as though I had thrown her a lifeline. She burst into tears and hugged me… thanked me…

I can't begin to describe the feeling that came over me. I, in my bereaved pitiful state, had been able to help another. Looking back, I believe that one positive action helped me as much as it did her.

For me, it was a beginning…

And this is what this organisation, The Compassionate Friends, is all about. In the words of our lovely present Chair, Maria Ahern: 'When you first start climbing the hill of grief you grasp the hand held out to you by someone further up and you hold on for dear life. In time you begin to hold out your own hand to help support someone struggling further down. And so it goes on…

And TCF goes on……

COPING WITH EVERYDAY LIFE

'Start by doing what is necessary. Then do what
is possible. And suddenly you're doing the
impossible.'
Saint Francis of Assisi

MORNING

**Where would we be without our first cup of tea in the
morning** - ok, or our first cup of coffee. Hauling myself out
of bed and reaching for my dressing gown, the one worn by
my daughter, then stumbling downstairs to put the kettle on,
It's another day without you in it.

Yawning, I reach for the mug, stick in the tea bag and
pour on the boiling water. I can't think straight yet but at
least I'm upright... well, until I can get to my comfy chair.
Add milk then sugar. Thank goodness I've moved the salt
away to another cupboard. At least now I can be certain it's
sugar I'm spooning in. Then I make my way to my chair.

My chair is next to the patio window looking out onto
the garden with its apple tree in the middle of the lawn. I
sink into it. Well at least I've accomplished one thing this
morning - getting up. I pat myself metaphorically on the
back. I could still be lying in bed willing myself to get up and
not managing it. I take a first sip of hot delicious soothing
caffeine and lean back in my chair...

My Chair
It wraps me round
my chair,
a padded garden chair
nobody wanted
but oh, so comfy

It wraps me round
in the morning,
hugs me safe
as I face
days
without you

It wraps me round
as I sip my tea
remembering,
as I sit
still
remembering,
wrapped up in you

Life is easier now, but I still think of those days in the past when I didn't want to get out of bed at all. The effort it was to get dressed. I didn't care what I wore. It was all so irrelevant. I remember the effort it was to put one foot in front of the other... just not wanting to go on but having to. It was then I remembered that invaluable saying:

'One foot in front of the other,
And don't forget to breathe.'

And now, I'm going to try getting on with life.

I'm going to:
- Get dressed
- Find something lurking in the fridge I can have for dinner
- Wash the things I meant to wash yesterday
- Send a card to my niece saying I'm sorry I missed her birthday
- Buy a loaf of bread and some milk

- Remember to laugh at myself, it's better than being angry

That's enough to be going on with…

I am trying NOT to think of all the things I've got to do this week. All that does is to stop me in my tracks.

I MUST REMEMBER:
We don't have to face the future all at once. We live it day by day. 'Don't try to face the whole year ahead or even next week. Face today and when that's done, face tomorrow.'

The Chinese have a saying, '**You begin a thousand mile journey with a single step**'. So if you're really struggling, start by doing one little thing: remember to breathe, then put one foot in front of the other until you reach the bread bin, find the toaster and the butter. Eat.

Pat yourself on the back; you have made a start, you have taken the first step.

HAVE YOU BEEN ASKED THAT DREADED QUESTION, 'HOW MANY CHILDREN DO YOU HAVE?' I certainly have. When I was waiting at the bus stop, chatting casually to a stranger to pass the time, out it came. I was instantly speechless… What on earth should I say? I just wanted the bus to come along and swallow me up.

CAN I HAVE AN EASIER QUESTION?
by Maureen Hunter, Mother of Stuart, TCF Mandurah
*One questions that instils horror and paralysis into the heart of any grieving parent is, '**How many children do you have?**' It seems such an innocent question to many, bandied about in general conversation and one we ourselves would have asked countless times; but everything is different now and I don't know about you but I want an easier question. I had thought about how I would answer that for the first time after Stuart*

died, I had it all sorted in my mind, how it would happen, what I would say… but the reality was far from my imaginings.

One night I got something in my eye, it wouldn't budge. With eyes streaming and one eye half shut I had to go to the local hospital for after hours' treatment. I had been there only three weeks before, in the very same room, when my son was taken there initially after his accident. I remembered everything but I was stoical: I was coping. But then the nurse, whilst 'fixing' my eye said, 'How many children do you have?'

Instantly my eyes welled up with tears and I became totally speechless. This was the very first time anyone had asked me that since Stuart died and I couldn't respond: no words would come out and I was totally overwhelmed with the impact the question had on my very being.

It's happened many times since then and now I have a bit of a repertoire up my sleeve. Circumstances will dictate what I say, whether I play it safe and say, 'I have three children', or whether I tell the whole story and elaborate. It all depends on who's asking, the relationship I have with them and the social situation I am in. It depends how I feel emotionally. Sometimes I don't have the inner strength to go into details, to add that little bit more, so I keep it brief for my own sake. That's just how it is. But for me, it's always three. I have three children, always have and always will have.

***

I don't know about you but I got used to putting on a 'brave face' when I was with other people. 'Oh, I'm alright', I'd say to questions as to how I was getting on. I'm sure they just wanted me to say that and then they could move on to the next topic. If I told them how I was really feeling, the tears would come out and I didn't want people to feel awkward or to wonder what on earth they could do to 'fix it'.

Masques

In idle conversation
you ask me about
my children.
You are an acquaintance.
I do not know you well
and so I don a masque,
I speak happily of joys,
light-heartedly of mischief,
but I do not speak
of death.

I do not want to see
the shadow of uncertainty
pass your face.
And feel the
awkward silence that falls
like a curtain between us.
I do not want to say,
'It's okay, that was
a long time ago.'
It will never be quite 'okay'
and sometimes it seems
like yesterday.

And so I take my masque
along with me through life
like a perpetual Halloween night,
to hide just a bit from people
and to preserve my strength.
For mourning is tiring
and each time I recount
that day of death,
I am a little wearied.

I would much rather speak
of the joys of his life
than the sorrows of his death,
to strangers
who absently ask
of children.

Yet tragedy is more universal
than ever I had known
before it touched my life.
And so at times I wonder
who else looks out from behind
a masque.

Karen Nelson, *TCF Box Elder County, USA*

We all cope with everyday life as best we can. At first we probably don't see the point in 'coping'. We just want to curl up and let life get on without us. After the funeral is over, and the weeks go by, people expect us to 'get back to normal'. I just wanted to sit in the garden and only get up to put the kettle on. But gradually I did make a start, repeating those words to myself over and over: 'One foot in front of the other, And don't forget to breathe.'

GRIEF

*'Grief never ends... but it
changes... Grief is not a sign of
weakness, nor a lack of
faith... it is the price of love.'*
Darcie Sims

I knew now I wasn't alone but I still carried the weight of the loss of my daughter, Nikki, round with me. Life had totally changed, I felt I was living on a different planet to everyone else. People were crossing the road going to the swimming baths near us and going into the shop to buy crisps and newspapers. How could they go on doing that? Life had stopped.

Then there were people visiting, arrangements for the funeral, the funeral itself… Then having to resume everyday life, get the children off to school; the days, weeks went by… And as the weeks went by I began, if anything, to feel even worse. People were expecting me to get 'back to normal' but how could I, when my life had been shattered.

'It won't always be like this', I was told. 'You WILL get through it.' I didn't believe them. But looking back now, I know they were right.

Jill Yglesias' vivid account of how it was at first, will, I'm sure, resound with many of you.

LOOKING BACK…
by Jill Yglesias
Recently I got out the journal I kept that first Christmas and re-read it for the first time in ten years. It was a stark black-and-white reminder of those stricken early days, weeks and months, when the pain was so raw, so visceral, the body and mind so

leaden and heart-broken, that we could barely function at all.

We were plunged into deep grief after the sudden death of our middle daughter Chloe, in August that year. She was driving along a country road to the local swimming-pool to collect her 9 year old son, JJ, and his friend, when her car swerved, hit a huge tree-stump, and overturned.

We cancelled the annual neighbourhood Carol concert that we always used to host at our house, but we still attempted to 'do' Xmas, as all the immediate family, including Chloe's husband and JJ, and our other two small grandchildren, were coming to stay.

On the first Xmas Eve I wrote:

'Terrible day. Grief-stricken from the kernel of me. Surges of deep despair and pain, welling up in sobbing and groaning. Stomach tight and gripping. Cannot cope. Cannot complete the simplest thing. Everything takes ages, and even then I stop and start and can hardly get to the end.' I couldn't even finish filling the stockings, and I had so little energy that I couldn't even manage to push the presents down into the stockings!

For a normally competent busy person, like me, the grief had the added burden of me feeling I wasn't on top of things! It forced me to accept that I was not in control.

Alice, my daughter, kept saying, 'Mum, this is normal, you're in grief, this is what happens, people can't focus, they've got no energy, they are fragile and tearful… don't give yourself a hard time; if you had cancer and were having chemo, no-one would expect you to be on top of it.'

We had absolutely no energy, no focus in between the crying and the feeling of disbelief. It was a monumental effort to cook, *or bake, or do anything, and each day felt like wading through treacle, our feet so heavy, our bodies so leaden and lethargic.*

We found what really helped was having the family around, because we were all going through it together. These constant waves of grief were passed like a 'sobbing baton' amongst us, so there were always people around to hug and support the crying one. In that we were blessed.

At one point, Alice - hearing a song her sister Chloe loved - broke down into shaking sobs. Her little boy, Finn, tried to push her away, shouting, 'Stop crying mummy, stop!' Alice said, 'I can't Finn, I can't.' We had to hold them both tight, telling Finn that it was ok to cry, mummy was missing Chloe so much.

Re-reading my words of anguish written at the time, I remember how physically and mentally exhausting grief is. Your life is ripped apart and fractured, and you can - quite simply - not function normally at all.

We need people to support us by 'holding' us and allowing us to cry, if that's how we feel, because tears are healing, they soften the tension of the body, which is tight with grief.

We need people to let us know that that is how it is; it is normal to feel like this, and it is alright. That's why being with other bereaved parents, for example at Compassionate Friends meetings, was for me an absolute lifeline, whereas my husband preferred to be at home, just with family. For many, many months I simply sat and cried throughout the meetings, feeling totally accepted by the group. This was a place where I could talk and cry about Chloe knowing that everyone there understood and had been through it too.

Everyone will find their own way to cope with the devastation of loss. Our way wasn't consciously chosen, it was just what happened - we needed to talk a lot and cry A LOT! quite openly within the family and with close friends.

Grief is tough work, but, one faltering step at a time, it does get less tsunami-like as time goes on. As Alice says, 'We managed to get through those darkest days and to find laughter and joy again, even though the sorrow will always be there, and the tears will fall at unexpected times.'

(You can read Jill's poem, *'Just Making the Gravy'*, in the Chapter on Christmas)

***

'Grief is not a disorder, a disease or a sign of weakness. It is an emotional, physical and spiritual necessity. The price you pay for love. The only cure for grief is to grieve.'   Earl Grollman

***

I can think of no better writer than Darcie Sims to outline the truth of grief and the choices we have to make.

CHOICE POINTS IN YOUR GRIEF
by Darcie Sims
We have always had choices in our lives:

- *Should I smile or cry now?*
- *Which thumb to suck?*
- *Which shoe to lose?*
- *Who will be my best friend?*
- *Who will be my second best friend?*
- *Which to eat first... dessert or vegetables?*
- *Which one to fall in love with?*
- *Whom to marry?*
- *How many children to have?*
- *What will we name them?*

And then, one day, we ran out of choices, or so we thought. Our world came to pieces, and the sky grew dark, and the sun went out. But even then, in the darkest moments that we have ever known, there were choices to be made... even if we did not recognise them. From the moment we learned of the death, there were choices to be made:

- *Should I continue breathing?*
- *Who needs to be notified?*
- *Which funeral home to use?*
- *Burial or cremation?*
- *Which clothes, music, readings?*
- *Who will do what?*
- *Should I continue breathing?*

In a world where there are no choices to be made, we are faced with countless choices that are required. Yet there is simply no energy, no brain power, no motivation to make any of them. We would prefer to lie down and die...and some of us tried, but it didn't work, and so we got up, dusted ourselves off, got busy, made coffee, tossed in a load of laundry, and began to move forward into grief... a world filled with choices we did not want to make!

In the early hours, days, weeks, and even months of grief, our choices are pretty basic and limited. We plod through the fog, frozen as icicles or Popsicles, functioning, but not feeling. It is early grief, and fortunately, the choices are pretty basic:

- *Should I eat?*
- *Should I go to work?*
- *Should I pay the bills?*
- *Should I keep breathing?*

But as grief progresses, our choices begin to become more complex:

- *What should we do with the stuff?*
- *What do we do with the room?*
- *Should I keep breathing?*
- *Should we move, stay married, hide?*
- *What do we tell everyone when they ask how we are?*
- *Why are we still breathing?*

Eventually, grief settles down into a routine of sorts... a new normal for us; and still there are choices to be made:

- *Should we go to a support group?*
- *Should I make him/her go with me?*
- *How should we memorialise our child/grandchild?*
- *How long should we be grieving?*
- *Can we move on, get over it, or stay in sadness forever?*

And finally, what should we bring with us into our new life?

- *Bitterness?*
- *Sadness?*
- *Guilt?*
- *Joy?*
- *Hate?*
- *Sorrow?*
- *Pain first?*
- *Pain always?*

You will wrestle long and hard, and finally discover the awful truth of grief: your child, your grandchild, your sibling, has died. You have not. You are left among the living, to carve out an existence that has to endure not only the pains of life but the joys as well. And suddenly, survival isn't enough. If you are to be stuck in life, then you can choose to live again.

We can choose how we wish grief to influence us. We can carry bitterness and anger, or we can choose to remember the light and the love. We rearrange the furniture, change rooms, and sometimes we move.

'The Room' becomes a den, a sewing room, a guest room, or perhaps someone else's room. We slowly begin to understand that putting our child's things away does not mean putting him or her out of our life.

This becomes a fork in the road . . . a choice point between grieving forever and learning to live with what you've got instead of what you wanted. You don't have to remember only the awfulness of the death. You can choose to recall the joys, the light your loved one brought, the music of his or her presence in your life:

These are the Choice Points in Grief:

You can choose what you remember.

You can choose what you carry with you. You can choose what you let go.

You can choose to carry hurt, pain, bitterness, and anger.

You can choose to carry joy, love, laughter, and life.

How long are you going to let the death overshadow the life?

Didn't say goodbye? Then say it now, or choose to say, ' love you,' now, tonight, and forever.

You don't stop loving someone just because they died.

You can choose whether you remember the death or the life first. You can look for joy and carry rose-colored glasses, or you can carry the pain and sorrow of the death. Risk it all; don't wait for anything anymore… just start dancing. Even if there is no light, our memory can light the way. No one can take our memories away. You can toss them away or give them away, but no one can destroy those precious moments of light. They will last forever.

Love is the size of a sigh
Light as a kiss
Gentle as a whisper
Small as a moment in time

I am glad I bought the ticket. I'm glad I paid the price. I am glad I shared the journey, and I have a memento or two from the ride. Let go of the hurt so there is room for love to grow. Remember the life, not just the death.

I think the truly bereaved are those who have never known love at all. You and I are rich beyond measure because someone loved us and we loved them… we still do. And for this I am thankful.

Grief isn't a seasonal song.
It's a lifetime song, but it doesn't have to be a sad song forever. Our loved ones lived. We loved them. We still do. I choose joy and thanks for the little while.

***

WE ALL NEED TO GRIEVE. If we don't allow ourselves to grieve, if we try to repress the dreadful pain of our child's death and busy ourselves so we don't have to feel anything, we are not allowing ourselves to begin to heal.

> **Grieving allows us to heal,**
> *to remember with love*
> *rather than pain.*
> *It is a sorting process.*
> *One by one you let go*
> *of the things that are gone*
> *and you mourn for them.*
> *One by one you take hold*

of the things that have
become a part of who you are
and build again.

Rachel Naomi Remen

GRIEVING IS DOING
Extract from the film, 'Say their Name', made for TCF by Jane Harris and Jimmy Edmonds

'There's a lot about grieving that's doing. It's not just feeling dreadful in a dark room. If you **do** stuff you **express** stuff; it's active and that's when you move forward in grief - when you express your love, because grief is about love.

'No one can tell you what you need to do because it's about your love and your unique relationship with that person who's died. Only you can possibly find the right symbols, or metaphors, or things... that express that. No one can lecture you... You can't read a book that tells you; it comes from within.

'And that's why when I see siblings that are very wrapped up in their parents' grief I respect it and know where they are. When you move forward is when you find the thing that expresses your grief. And that's important to do.'

***

Some of you have also done, or are doing, or will do in the future, something that expresses your grief and your love: creating a quilt out of your child's clothes, setting up a charity in your child's name, running to raise money for TCF and other charities of your choice, writing poems, keeping a grief diary and many other things.

Some of you, as the years have gone by, have become TCF volunteers who take on essential roles like running the helpline, being a contact, running groups, weekends, training days, running our office and our postal library. Grieving is doing and all these activities express your grief and your love.

Have **you** found something you can do that expresses your grief and love for your child, grandchild or sibling?

A FATHER'S GRIEF

*'If you're embarrassed because you have some
notion about how men are supposed to behave,
and it doesn't include weeping, then you have some
personal work to do.'*
Ray Bradbury

**When our daughter, Nikki died, my husband and I were
both overwhelmed by grief.** I wanted to sit with a friend
drinking cups of tea, talking, being hugged and listened
to. My husband put all his physical and emotional energy
into raising money to buy a harp for the Music Centre in
High Wycombe, where our daughter had played clarinet
in an orchestra. Two very different ways of reacting to the
traumatic death of our daughter.

Jimmy Edmonds puts this very clearly in his poem:

Some Words for Father's Day
Jimmy and Jane's son, Josh, died at the age of 22
Fathers don't grieve like mothers do
Fathers don't hurt like mothers do
Fathers don't yearn for a lost child like their partner will
*Fathers are quite good at pretending that everything is
    OK…ish*
I've seen some fathers cry while their friends turn away
*but I've never seen a father howl in anguish and cling
    to another*
because the pain is too great
*My father is now a distant memory. He taught me how
to bear life's punishments but not to bare my soul*
He would disapprove if I shared my son's death
and talked about him as if he were still alive.

What's past is past he would say
and he would know because he fought a war
and saw many comrades fall
Life is for living was his constant refrain
and in a way he was right
But then I didn't die before him
Did I?

Jimmy Edmonds

It doesn't matter who we are, we all need to share our grief - dads as well as mums:

BOXING IS A MAN'S GAME
by Tom Crouthamel, TCF Sarasota FL

'Ladies and gentlemen! In the right corner weighing in at 10,000 pounds, fighting bare knuckled, undefeated in millions of fights, GRIEF! GRIEF! And in the left corner, fighting for the first time in his life, wearing six ounce gloves, YOU! YOU! There is no three knockdown rule, no standing seven count and the fight continues till YOU is dead. Shake hands and come out fighting!'

As a bereaved father, you are in the worst and most uneven fight of your life. You can do it all alone or you can have some experienced trainers and managers in your corner. Take your choice! You wouldn't climb into the ring with Sugar Ray or Ali without all the help you could beg, borrow or steal. So why do you think that you can fight the most experienced, the most savvy, the dirtiest and most vicious fighter man has ever faced, all by yourself?

By coming to support meetings, you'll meet other bereaved fathers who have fought GRIEF *and they can advise you in your fight. No, they won't get into the ring with you, but they can tell you how to bob and weave, when to duck and hold,* *how to grab and strike back.*

They can help to staunch cuts, they can recall strategies that worked for them, and if necessary, they can help you call in the ring physician. Of course you can fight it all alone, it is your choice.

The fight never ends. Finally GRIEF becomes tired and the bout turns to an uneasy truce. GRIEF can still throw out a jab that will knock you to the canvas. But with friends in your corner, your eyes can clear faster and you can get up quicker.

With good handlers the uneasy truce stage arrives sooner, but it is your choice! You can stay home and never go to a meeting or talk with another dad. GRIEF vs YOU. How long do you want to fight alone?

DADS' GROUP AT A TCF RESIDENTIAL WEEKEND
by Jimmy Edwards
What I like about the fathers' groups at TCF is that they aren't so much about trying to find answers to problems (or trying to fix things). More they are simply an opportunity to remove the mask and just be who we are - dads who are desperately trying to come to terms with the death of our child and to accommodate it into the rest of our lives.

For most this is stuff we have never done before. We didn't learn how to mourn as kids, grief is not on any school curriculum, and everything we learn about being a man and a dad leaves us totally unprepared for death, least of all the death of our child.

I see the fathers' groups at TCF as a kind of bubble where we can learn from each other and practice expressing our grief in a safe environment, all the better to deal with what may or may not be conscious insensitivities of the outside world.

As one dad said, 'More than anything it was an occasion where I made friends with several bereaved dads and I aim to keep in touch with them. I learnt that there is light at the end of the tunnel.'

***

If we remain silent, or if we immerse ourselves in activities to occupy our time, our partner may not realise just how much we are grieving. It is important for us to be aware of the need to express our grief in different ways and to allow each other to do this.

REAL MEN DO CRY
by Carrie Kears, TCF Otago
On January 1996 my life was forever changed when my brother, Carl, died. Time stood still as I listened in disbelief as I was told how he was found at the bottom of a radio tower. I sought to escape my thoughts by watching television, such brief respites from my pain were not only necessary, but few and far between.

As I walked into the television den, I caught my father sitting on the edge of the couch in the grip of his own painful moment of grief. I could see him facing the stark realisation that his son would never again walk through the door, ask to go deep sea fishing, try to weasel a couple of bucks before rushing out of the door.

I sat quietly down beside him, not quite knowing if he would be receptive or embarrassed by my presence. I slipped an arm up over his shoulder, which began to shake silently before my arm could even come to rest. The silent shakes of his shoulders gave way to heart-wenching, gut-churning, whole-body sobs. I reached up across his chest to grasp his opposite shoulder and lowered my cheek onto the shoulder nearest to me, feeling his tears fall across my forearm. I couldn't tell you how long we sat there sharing our tears, our pain.

It was the first time I had ever seen my father truly break down, the first time I witnessed something more than a single stoic tear trickle down his cheek. As I look back on the experience I recognise it as a turning point in our relationship. His intense pain did not create for me a greater burden in my grief. I was not frightened. My world did not cave in because my father allowed me to see him grieve. In all honesty **my world was enriched because my father not only allowed me to see him grieve, he allowed me to grieve with him,** beside him in a moment which laid the foundation of our current relationship. His actions let me know it is alright for me to allow myself to feel pain, and to share it with my family.

I do not hesitate to call my parents or show up at their doorstep when I am desperately missing Carl, or grieving the loss of our unrealised future. I desperately want Carl to know my daughter, to be an uncle to her just as much as I desperately desire to be an aunt to the children he will never have. Grief is not only missing what was, but missing what would have been. I am grateful to my father for showing me I am not alone in my grief. Only time can lessen the pain of grief, but my pain is more bearable when I share my grief. I have grown up with knowledge of people who believe real men don't cry.

Maybe they haven't lost a son. Maybe they haven't had the chance to be an example to the daughters who share the grief. As General Schwarzkopf said when asked if he was afraid to cry, 'I'm afraid of any person who won't cry.'

***

HUGH McANINCH, A BEREAVED DAD AND MEMBER OF TCF WRITES...

Very often I hear and read from those who have lost a child about the terrible misunderstandings they face that are created with family, relations, friends and work colleagues. In some instances they have led to a complete breakdown in relationships.

Those who have not lost a child do not understand who we are or how we feel anymore, but how could they possibly anyway? Losing a child is beyond anyone's comprehension until...

If we could simply leave them with our wish list they would have a better understanding. This is my Wish List but it could be yours too. I hope it helps.

My Wish List

- *I wish you would not be afraid to speak my loved one's name. They lived and were very important and I need to hear their name.*

- *If I cry and get emotional if we talk about my loved ones, I wish you knew you haven't hurt me. The fact that they died causes my tears. You have allowed me to cry and I thank you. Crying and emotional outbursts are healing.*

- *I will have emotional highs and lows, ups and downs. I wish you wouldn't think that if I have a good cry my grief is over, or that if I have a bad day I need psychiatric counselling.*

- *Being a bereaved parent is not contagious, so I wish you wouldn't stay away.*

- *I wish you knew all the 'crazy' reactions that I am*

having are in fact very normal. Depression, anger, fear, hopelessness and questioning of values and beliefs are to be expected following a death.

- I wish you wouldn't expect my grief to be over in six months. The first few years are going to be exceedingly traumatic for me. As with alcoholics I will never be 'cured' or 'formerly bereaved' but forevermore be recovering from my bereavement.

- I wish you understood the physical reaction to grief. I may gain weight, lose weight, sleep all the time, or not at all, develop a host of illnesses and be accident prone, all of which are related to my grief.

- Our loved one's birthday, the anniversary of their death and the holidays are terrible times for us. I wish you could tell us that you are thinking of us on these days. If we get quiet and withdrawn, know that we are thinking about them and don't coerce us into being cheerful.

- I wish you wouldn't offer to take me out for a drink or to a party. This is just a temporary crutch and the only way I can get through this grief is to experience it. I have to hurt before I can heal.

- I wish you understood that grief changes people. I am not the same person I was before my loved one died. If you keep waiting for me to 'get back to my old self' you will stay frustrated. I am a new person with new thoughts, dreams, aspirations, values and beliefs. Please get to know me - maybe you'll still like me.

***

'It takes a strong man to be a father and an even stronger man to be a grieving father.'

POST TRAUMATIC STRESS DISORDER (PTSD)

When my daughter, Nikki, died, I thought I would never survive. I didn't want to wake up in the morning. I didn't want to go through another day without her. I sat in the garden, hour after hour, doing nothing. I had a book but I couldn't read, I couldn't even attempt to concentrate. And my feelings, my thoughts, so strong, so bizarre… Everything was unreal, I was living in another world. I thought I was going mad…

But I wasn't. What I had was an absolutely natural reaction to sudden trauma, to the death of my child. We parents, grandparents and siblings who are suddenly or traumatically bereaved are also enveloped in massive Post Traumatic Stress Disorder, and the symptoms which hit us are not simply the effects of our massive grief but the result of PTSD.

When my son, Robin, died, 16 years later, from encephalitis, I was again hit by bizarre thoughts and feelings but this second time round I understood what was happening to me and knew that it would pass.

I learnt about Post Traumatic Stress Disorder from a speech given by Dr Margaret Brearley at one of our TCF residential weekends. Here, in a slightly shortened version, is her informative and inspiring speech.

TRAUMATIC GRIEF by Margaret Brearley
Woodbrooke 11-13th July 2016
All loss is traumatic. But to lose a son or daughter is the most devastating loss - and profoundly traumatic, especially if sudden or violent or complicated. Self-inflicted deaths, or

deaths inflicted by addiction or substance use, bring additional trauma to parents and other surviving family members.

When our Joshua died, suddenly and out of the blue, I felt as though I was going mad with grief. I often felt like driving into a wall or leaping in front of a tube train - even now I stand well back from the platform, in case of a sudden mad impulse. For months my mind continually 'searched' for Joshua, thinking that I spotted him in the distance, and for years I constantly had flashbacks of when I found Joshua dead in bed, the Sunday before Christmas 2002.

As I got to know more and more newly bereaved parents both within TCF and outside, I noticed that apparently odd behaviour is normal among us. Several of my new friends would go out in their cars to scream. Two bereaved mothers could not leave their homes for a year. Another could not remain in her home in daylight for a year and a half, due to her extreme restlessness.

Because I had many friends who were Holocaust survivors, I knew that odd behaviour can be a reaction to extreme trauma. I had known an elderly survivor from Germany who shook and broke into a run whenever he saw a cross; others always carried bread with them, because of past starvation.

All bereaved parents are to a greater or lesser degree traumatised. This is why Anna Bonham-Carter, mother of our Joshua's friend, Sebastian, who died eighteen months before Joshua, had rushed to befriend us as soon as she heard of Joshua's death. She had learnt, she explained, that, 'One must run towards bereaved parents', to comfort and support them in the intensity of their immediate grief and shock.

For our anguish as newly bereaved parents is heart-rending, immense and complex. The death itself of our son or daughter is traumatic - but so, too, is the inquest. Traumatic, too, is our anger if our child was let down by CAMS or their

GP or psychiatrists or others.

Bereaved parents suffer multiple trauma. Our world has changed overnight. Many experience isolation due to the loss of family and friends; the loss of financial security if one or both parents cannot work for a time; the loss of a close relationship with partner or spouse. It can feel like multiple amputation, with so much rupture.

Other aspects of one's child's death can also be traumatic; *coping with funeral expenses or one's child's digital legacy; the inability of others to comprehend our grief and their sometimes foolish comments; the loss of psychic security - everything now seems deeply unstable after the unthinkable has actually occurred.*

Waves of grief can come, utterly unexpectedly, and times formerly approached with keen anticipation - school holidays, anniversaries, birthdays - can now fill one with dread. If one has experienced previous trauma or the deaths of close family or dear friends, the new catastrophe can redouble one's sense of loss and deep distress. The poet Elizabeth Jennings, has written:

> *'Grief can return without warning...*
> *...Time does not heal,*
> *It makes a half-stitched scar*
> *That can be broken and again you feel*
> *Grief as total as in its first hour'.*

Emotions can be extremely strong and hard to cope with *- anger, remorse, a sense of often totally unjustified guilt - all assail bereaved parents. And however capable one was before the death, some things can seem almost impossible to cope with because of their emotional content - especially dealing with one's child's belongings, room, clothes or ashes.*

A couple of years ago I read a fascinating book - 'Aftermath: Violence and the Remaking of the Self'. It was by

Susan Brison, an American philosopher who, after she had survived being severely beaten, raped, strangled to near death and hospitalised for many months, found that long after the attack she still suffered from flashbacks, shaking, panic attacks, and other forms of irrational and compulsive behaviour. As a result, she decided to research the impact of sudden trauma on other survivors of violent assault and the PTSD associated with it.

Reading this book was what made me realise that we parents, who are suddenly or traumatically bereaved, are also assaulted by massive PTSD *- and that the symptoms which hit us and can linger for years, are not simply the effects of massive grief but are actually the result of post-traumatic stress disorder.*

Here are the three core symptoms of PTSD after trauma as outlined by David Alexander and Susan Klein in their 2013 book, 'Grief, Loss and Bereavement':

- **Re-experiencing the trauma** (through intrusive memories, flashbacks and nightmares).
- **Avoiding reminders of the traumatic event** - including the scene of the event and people associated with it.
- **Hyper-arousal - extreme nerviness and being 'on edge':** irritability, sleep loss, being easily startled by sounds. Also hyper-vigilance - survivors have an exaggerated sense of risk.

There are other common symptoms of PTSD which seem deeply abnormal but which are in fact normal reactions to profound trauma. They include:

- **flashbacks** - *'seeing' again and again one's child's body or the scene of their death*
- **memory loss** - *'post-fatal' amnesia can be worse and longer-lasting than post-natal amnesia.*
- **repetitive actions,** *such as constant sighing, clutching*

one's chest, rubbing one's arm

feelings of intense loneliness, *even when surrounded by others*

feelings of being disconnected *from everyone and everything, of being somehow alien*

feeling that everything is unreal; *even the death of the loved one is unreal*

feeling that life is empty and meaningless

wanting to die

thinking that one is going mad

numbness - *the inability to feel or to cry*

despair

feeling shocked, dazed, stunned or emotionally dead

swift uncontrollable changes of mood - *sudden laughter or weeping*

dread on waking or on encountering new situations or entering new places

experiencing agoraphobia *(fear of going outside)*

extreme restlessness

finding it hard to care about or trust other people

insomnia

physical pain in the heart or stomach - *feeling that 'my heart is seared in two' can seem physically real*

Another symptom is **absentmindedness.** *Here is a poem by Gina Claye:*

Forgetting

No, my mind isn't on the job in hand
I freely admit it and
frequently I find myself, well,
not where I should be at all.

I've just not been sleeping
so I set off to get a prescription

but instead of going to the doctors
the car went to Tescos.

So I bought the milk I forgot yesterday.

I thought I'd sorted out probate
but there's yet more legal stuff to cope with.
Well, forget the solicitors
the car went to Tescos.

Wish I hadn't forgotten my mobile.

Tomorrow it's the dentist.
I've been putting it off since last August
I know I'll be shaking with fright
but with any luck and despite
my very best intentions,
the car will end up in Tescos.

*David Alexander and Susan Klein believe that PTSD symptoms
can interfere with grieving:*

> *through constantly re-experiencing traumatic images and
> memories of the death scene*

> *by becoming totally preoccupied with certain aspects of
> the death e.g. one's real or imagined contribution to the
> death*

> *by constantly avoiding reminders of the death or of the one
> who has died*

> *post-traumatic numbness 'may cause the bereaved to
> become distanced from individuals and circumstances
> that can be supportive and facilitate grieving'*

BE REASSURED: *If your today is marked by symptoms of PTSD, there will indeed be a different tomorrow when you will be free of them.*

PTSD often does not lessen if people are isolated. However, research has shown that both intense grief and acute PTSD symptoms do gradually disappear if one is part of a community, such as TCF, in which one can share one's loss and suffering. This is generally true of Holocaust survivors, torture survivors and survivors of other tragedies.

It is equally true of bereaved people when they can share and talk about their grief - with a counsellor or with other bereaved parents - ideally the sooner the better. Recent trauma research at Oxford has shown, for example, that staying up as late as possible and talking on the night of a tragedy helps lessen its impact. By and large, the sooner one can begin to talk about the trauma and to share one's anguish, the better.

WHAT HELPS US OVERCOME PTSD? *There is no magic bullet, but some things can definitely help:*

Confronting PTSD head-on *- not being afraid of symptoms such as flash-backs, but recognising them*

A course of talking therapy, bereavement counselling or Cognitive Behavioural Therapy (CBT) *can often help*

Accompaniment: *- a newly bereaved mother whose son had died in an accident couldn't stay in her house in daylight for well over a year - so other friends and I tried to take her out - window-shopping, walking, having coffee in cafes - anything to distract her from her overwhelming pain*

Recognising the symptoms as being the natural way *in which one's body or mind copes with unnatural levels of stress*

Naming one's fears; *in fairy tales evil figures (Rumpelstiltskin) lose their power once they are named*

Being listened to *- Helen Bamber, who founded the first British organisation to care for torture survivors, developed* *what she called 'divine inquisitiveness' - intent listening and gentle questioning which bring healing*

TAKE HEART, YOU DEAR FRIENDS. You will find that your symptoms of trauma - flashbacks or memory loss, numbness and despair and thinking you are going mad and wanting to die, feeling intensely lonely and that everything is unreal - these will gradually disappear.

Time really does help. Your anguish now is jagged, like a sharp flint in your body, piercing your heart and your soul. Gradually your grief will become like a smooth rounded pebble, always lodged within you but somehow bearable.

Your profound bond of love with your son or daughter, so cruelly snatched away and for whom you yearn incessantly, will continue: gradually he or she will feel closer and even a part of you, as you carry their treasured memory with you. Dennis Klass, who has studied the continuing bonds of parents with their dead sons or daughters, has written:

'Membership in a Compassionate Friends community means that the dead child is also a member of that community, that the child is valued, remembered, celebrated and loved...the children are the heart and soul of TCF.'

As one does things to honour one's child and tries to live by their and one's own best values, an inner conversation with them gradually develops and happy memories slowly begin to return.

Grief is hard work.

Grieving allows us slowly to forget how our beloved son or daughter died and to remember who they were before their death.

Grieving allows us to recapture their precious love for us and to keep alive our profound love for them. That mutual love never dies. This is how the poet Elizabeth Barrett Browning expressed undying love:

'How do I love thee? Let me count the ways.
I love thee to the depth and breadth and height
My soul can reach...I love thee with the breath,
Smiles, tears, of all my life! - and if God choose,
I shall but love thee better after death'.

Grieving allows us gradually to recall and honour our son's or daughter's unique, precious character and personality, so that their name will become a blessing to you and to others. All your life long you will be able to do good, creative things - some small, some larger, in your child's name. You maybe can't envisage it yet, but it will happen - again and again.

You will find that in some extraordinary way, our broken hearts gradually become open hearts, able to empathise with the pain of others because we ourselves know the pain of grief. Here is a paradox:

'Just as 'Nothing screams like silence', 'Nothing is so whole as a broken heart'.

Whenever negative thoughts come, remind yourself that you are a hero or heroine. You have shown courage in great adversity; you have struggled passionately to care for your beloved child through thick and thin, as no one else could.

Unexpected moments of joy will come. Just as your friends and family cannot imagine the depths of your pain and grief, so too you cannot imagine that you will ever again be happy or joyful. But although we are permanently scarred by grief, I know that, as you are comforted by friends both within and outside TCF, you will find joy again, tinged always by sorrow but eventually radiant with hope.

But for now, I beg you, pamper yourselves and those closest to you. Be kind to yourselves. Each day try to do something fun - see a good film or watch a comedy DVD, phone a friend for coffee or buy a new lipstick or tie or read a poem or walk in a wood or simply gaze at the sky and hear a tiny wren with its *heroic, thrilling song.*

Although bereft, you are not alone. We in the Compassionate Friends are an extended family who belong to one another. *And as you gradually open your heart to others, you will find that others will come to you, who need you.*

Here is The Gift by Joe Lawley, one of the bereaved parents who helped to found The Compassionate Friends fifty years ago:

The Gift
I have a gift.
I did not want this gift, it meant suffering and pain.
The pain came because of love.
A love which had manifested itself in a child.
The child brought its love to me and asked for my love.
Sometimes I did not understand this.
Sometimes I did not appreciate it.
Sometimes I was too busy to listen quietly to this love.
But the love persisted; it was always there.

One day the child died.
But the love remained.
This time the love came in other forms.
This time there were memories; there was sadness and
*   anguish.*
And unbelievable pain.

One day a stranger came and stood with me.
The stranger listened and occasionally spoke.
The stranger said 'I understand', and did.
You see the stranger had also been this way.
We talked and cried together.
The stranger touched me to comfort.
The stranger became my friend as no other had.
My friend said, 'I am always here', and was.

One day I lifted my head.
I noticed another grieving, grey and drawn with pain.
I approached and spoke.
I touched and comforted.
I said, 'I will walk with you', and did.

I also had the gift.

Joe Lawley

A parent's love is beyond death. You can still express your love by being kind and loving to yourself, your spouse or partner, to any beloved surviving children.

The spirit of your son, daughter or sibling lives on in each word, gesture, deed of kindness which you perform inspired by their memory and your love for them.

You in turn can reach out to comfort other traumatised bereaved parents through strengthening TCF - by fundraising or by giving your time or your listening skills.

There is a traditional saying that 'suffering shared by many is a partial comfort'. We in TCF can share one another's suffering. We can indeed comfort one another. A broken heart never fully mends. But a broken heart can create miracles. Here is a Jewish story:

> *'A messenger comes to the mourner's house. "Come", says the messenger, "you are needed".*
> *"I cannot come", says the mourner, "my spirit is broken".*
> *"That is why you are needed", says the messenger.'*

A broken heart can achieve a miracle of love. You wonderful, dear, heroic, broken-hearted, openhearted, warm-hearted parents - as you reach out to others, may you each achieve your own miracle of love.

***

THANK YOU MARGARET. I learned so much that day I listened to your speech. I wish I'd known, when I was first bereaved, that this trauma I was going through was normal and that it would pass. I do hope that those of you who are newly bereaved will draw comfort from knowing that what you are experiencing is a normal stage of traumatic grief and that these symptoms of PTSD will gradually lessen.

A friend of mine drew my attention to EMDR (Eye Movement Desensitisation and Reprocessing), a therapy to help cope with PTSD, and sent me the following:

HELPING TO COPE WITH PTSD
by Mary Hartley

EMDR (Eye Movement Desensitisation and Reprocessing) is a therapy to help those of us suffering from PTSD, to work through our traumatic thoughts and memories in order to find some peace of mind. It isn't a cure for PTSD, but it can help us to cope with it and learn to live again.

Two people who were helped by this therapy were Gemma and Sally Dowler, the sister and mother of Milly Dowler who was abducted and murdered. Talking to a conference on EMDR, her mother, Sally Dowler, talked about the way it had helped her:

'In my back garden I have a pergola which I built with my dad many, many years ago. Over the pergola is a beautiful yellow rose.' She goes on to explain how, when she looked at the rose, all she could see was the memory of policemen smoking and pacing up and down waiting for her husband to come home, before they broke the news that a body had been found.

EMDR therapy helped her to work through that memory and break through to the memories beneath it, so that, 'Out of the blue I began to remember actually planting that rose with the girls, and Milly watering it with her little yellow watering can... Now, when I look at that rose, I can see us planting it again and I feel nice.'

Gemma writes about this, and about the way EMDR has also helped her, in her book, 'My Sister Milly'.

ANGER AND GUILT

Yes, I'd Kick it where it Hurts...

If Life stood there in front of me
I'd punch it in the face,
I'd kick it where it hurts, and
Shout out for the human race.

'Take that and that and that!
Leave me and mine alone!
Oh, do please forgive me
My unusual bereavement tone!

'Well, I'll fight you all along the way,
And even if I lose
I'll leave you with a bloody nose
And you can try and mend
Your own bloody fuse!'

Angela Jukes
Written in the rage of the first year's bereavement

Thank goodness for cars! Have you gone into your car and, as you were driving along, shouted and screamed at the world. You haven't? Well, you're one of the very few. Your world has fallen apart. It's ok to feel angry, don't beat yourself up about it, and the car doesn't mind.

Remember, it's normal to feel angry at just about everything when you're grieving; these are a list of the things that you might get angry about - and know that you're not the only one.

THINGS THAT MAKE ME ANGRY
taken from a List compiled by Friends in TCF South Australia

Anger at those who don't want to talk about, or listen to us talk about, our dead child

Anger at people who fail to realise the depth of our loss

Anger at our helplessness over the situation

Anger at those who say the wrong things or, worse, those who say nothing

Anger because life is going on for everyone but us

Anger because nothing will ever be the same again

Anger at other parents who don't appreciate their own good fortune

Anger at well-meaning friends who say that all we need is to 'get involved in something new', or to 'stay busy' - or to 'have another baby'

Anger because religion doesn't help, and more anger because we feel that way

Anger because our partner is never grieving the same way as we are

Anger at the doctors and others who we feel could have saved our child

Anger because we have been 'singled out' for this tragedy

Anger at the perpetrator if the death was murder or a car accident

Anger at the judicial system and inefficiencies of police and official departments

Anger at the doctor who treated our child (if the child died from suicide) and didn't notice the degree of depression

Anger towards ourselves for not noticing that our child was suicidal

Anger at the doctors for not preparing us for our child's imminent death

Anger when family and friends ask us, 'Aren't you over it yet?'

I think it helps just to see them written down! Getting my

feelings down on paper, whatever they are, I find a great release.

MY MORNING PAGES
by Marion Cameron

In that first horrible waking moment when you are faced with the reality that your child is dead, my next thought was ANGER. I had to write down this anger and any other thoughts and feelings in my head for three pages at least.

I felt a sort of release, and I continued with these pages every morning for about six months... I never reread them.

***

And WHY this anger...?

THE ANGER OF BEREAVED PARENTS
by Denis Pye

The anger of bereaved parents can often be seen as a reaction to feelings of helplessness and loss of control over events. Our beloved child has died, whether suddenly through accident, suicide, substance use, murder, or as a result of illness and disease - and we have not been able to prevent it.

Our desperate frustration emerges in anger, either against particular others, against the whole world, or against God. Someone must be responsible, someone must be to blame for our loss, our suffering and our pain. So, our anger is directed against those seen to be responsible, or sometimes simply against those nearest to us. In this way, our anger may be turned on doctors and hospital staff, on police, or on the driver of the vehicle involved in our child's death.

Writers on bereavement have often mentioned the anger, conscious or submerged, which can exist against the loved one who has died. This can present an enormous problem to bereaved parents. How could we be angry with the daughter or son we have cherished so much? Yet many of us have experienced such feelings, unreasonable or unjustified though they may be. But we could, after all, be angry with our children when they were alive and still love them, couldn't we? Better, surely, that the anger is brought to the surface rather than repressed and added to our burden of unnecessary guilt.

The very worst outcome is that anger, unacknowledged and unexpressed after our child's death, is turned inwards against ourselves, gnawing away at our sense of self-worth and leading to the despair of deep depression.

We have all felt the beginnings of this descent in a temptation to blame ourselves. Like all the welter of emotions which hit us in the terrible weeks and months following our loss, it needs to be faced and talked out with those who will listen - with real empathy and understanding.

***

AND THEN THERE'S GUILT

After Nikki died I felt guilty. Surely I should have been able to do or say something which would have stopped her taking her life. I kept on and on thinking about how I could have handled things differently, until eventually I brought myself up short and started to think about what we did do.

After the first attempt we took her to see the doctor and various consultants. We made sure she knew how much we loved her exactly as she was. I thought of everything positive I could say to her. It made no difference. She died at the fifth attempt. I had gone out that evening and I felt very guilty about that even though she died in the early hours of the morning.

You can imagine what I said to myself. If only I hadn't gone out, I might have been able to put her in a different frame of mind. But you can't live like that... And then a friend told us that they had done all they could for twenty years to try to stop their daughter from taking her life... But finally she succeeded. Somehow, knowing that, helped me...

I started to read up about guilt and came across these words:

*'We may feel guilty and not understand why. We need to remind ourselves that **feeling guilty is a natural part of the grief process.** This is particularly true when we are grieving our children.'*

Catherine McNulty

To know that feeling guilty was a natural part of grieving, helped me, as did the thought that Nikki would certainly not want me to feel like this.

And so the Guilt passed... and I hope that, if you are going through the stage of feeling unbearable guilt, reading this will help, if just in a little way...

GRANDPARENTS

When our child dies we have our own grief to contend with but if our child had children then we take on board their grief too and do our best to support them.

It has long been accepted that continuing a relationship of memory with the deceased is a healthy way of processing grief. This applies to children also, who benefit greatly when they are supported in remembering their parent.

FINDING WHAT WORKS FOR US
by Ann Bray
My eldest daughter, Nikki, was 34 years old when she died from cancer on 25th June 2014. Her girls were then nine and seven years old.

The only thing that got me through that very dark time was caring for Nikki's girls. When Nikki died the girls and I did lots of Fundraising which was therapeutic but exhausting, I love sewing, knitting and crochet so we made lots of things together that our family and friends very kindly bought (even if they didn't want them!).

The girls and I have also taken part in Race for Life every year; training helps, running, or in my case walking.

Last year I found TCF by chance and my local group has been a godsend, but the TCF Library is what helps me the most. I used to be an avid reader and Nikki and I belonged to a book group. After she died I couldn't read anything, I explained this to Mary Hartley at the library and she selected some books she thought would be helpful. Well, I devoured them and have been doing so regularly since I joined.

Another thing we have done as a family is place a commemorative bench in a beautiful spot where my children spent many hours and all of my grandchildren play and walk now. It has a little plaque dedicating it to Nikki and we can go there whenever we want.

I think we all just have to find our own way and what works for us.

***

HELPING OUR GRANDCHILDREN REMEMBER

There are many ways in which grandparents can help children remember their parent. We could make a memory book with our grandchildren or put together a memory box which can include photographs, newspaper stories, a family tree and treasured items.

This could be a great help to our grandchildren whose own memories of their parent will fade over the years. Something as simple as telling our grandchildren stories about when their mother or father was young can also help them, although we might not be ready to do this at the earliest time of our grief, when we ourselves are feeling very emotional. Grandparents need to grieve too!

Another positive activity can be helping them to make cards for Mother's or Father's Day and the birthday of their deceased parent. We might also help them do the same for their surviving parent to help build the relationship between the whole family.

STAYING IN TOUCH

If your grandchildren are living at some distance from you, you can keep in touch by sending cards and gifts on birthdays and at Christmas and other festivals. Cards, letters, text messages and emails can be sent at any time. Phone them up or set up a webcam link (especially useful if they live a long way away or have moved to another country). In this way you can reassure them that your relationship with them is important.

LIFE AFTER MY GRANDCHILD DIED
by Iris Hodgson

My 14 year old granddaughter, Erin, passed on, in 2014. My Christian faith helped me enormously at that time, without it I do not think I could have coped; it still sustains me every day and will for the rest of my days. Since Erin died I have made a big effort to appreciate life more, as sadly I know how fragile life is.

I try not to waste a precious moment worrying but try to be more positive and complain less. I also try to eat more healthily and exercise more: I garden and I walk.

A lot of the words I used to use very flippantly, such as, boring, routine, fine, depressed, fed up etc, take on a different meaning now. In this wonderful world I never allow myself to be bored; routine is good and better than tragedy. I no longer use the word, 'fine'. I say, 'I am good'. I don't say 'depressed' anymore as I'm not. I no longer say 'fed up' as there is so much I am able to do that sadly Erin can't.

I include Erin in my life journey by speaking to her about where I am, how I feel - silly things and serious things. This keeps her memory alive and keeps me close to her.

On the Anniversary of Erin's passing my grandchildren write a message on a balloon and put it on Erin's tree in the garden, and on her birthday we have a Birthday Meal in a restaurant and lift our glasses for a toast.

I feel that to use the precious gifts I have been given such as my body, my intellect, my characteristics to the best of my ability is honouring my lovely granddaughter. I have changed forever since my loss, and became a better person who appreciates life more. This is my granddaughter, Erin's legacy.

***

WHEN OUR GRANDCHILD DIES
Taken from a leaflet produced by TCF and which can be accessed on our website at www.tcf.org.uk

The death of a grandchild is a double burden for us: at the same time as grieving as a grandparent, we have to find the strength to support our son or daughter. We feel great sorrow, not only at the loss of our grandchild, but also at the impact of the gap it has left in our family.

Many grandparents suffer from feelings of guilt. We are alive when someone, much younger than us, has died. We may wish that we had died in their place: the death of a child, let alone a grandchild, is against the natural order.

Helping our child
The best support is often being available to listen and empathise while they share their anger, anguish and despair with us.

We can offer to help with the practical demands of family life, such as in the care of other grandchildren who will be grieving also, and may be feeling very left out. Looking after any family pets, or perhaps doing a little work around the house, can relieve some of the pressures on our daughter or son; it is important to remember to pace ourselves so that we do not get overtired. We need to cope with our own grief and find time to replenish our energies.

Helping our other grandchildren

If there are surviving grandchildren in the bereaved family, we may find that we are able to offer them much needed stability, comfort and support, especially while the usual patterns of family life are disrupted.

Brothers and sisters of the dead child will have many fears and worries at this time. It is common for them to dread that they too might die, especially if their sibling died of an illness. We must try to answer their questions as simply and honestly as possible, even though this is painful and difficult for them and us. TCF publishes leaflets and articles on children's grief and their changing understanding of death as they grow older. Our TCF Postal Library has a range of literature that may be helpful.

Hope

Over the years, the pain and problems of our early grief as grandparents will hopefully lessen in intensity. The support and understanding of others, who have endured similar experiences and are further along the journey of grief, can be of comfort to us. Eventually, we will be able to look back and remember the happy times we spent with our grandchildren and be glad that they lived, albeit that their lives were cut short.

SIBLINGS

SUPPORT FOR SIBLINGS
by Hayley Hayes
1 Online Support

What's unique about online support is its offer of reassurance that however crippling your grief may feel, you aren't alone. There is always somebody who will listen and empathise - 24/7. If you are feeling down on a Friday night, struggling on a Monday morning, or a challenging thought or even an uplifting memory pops into your head - you have a safe space in which to share it that very instant. More often than not, a post will be seen and responded to on our Facebook group very quickly. This can really help to alleviate the loneliness that so often comes with grief.

For some of us, the physical distance offered by being the other side of a screen helps us feel less inhibited and more able to share. Another way online support can help is by enabling ongoing, regular communication between those who may not be able to attend a regular 'real world' support group. It encourages a sense of community and also facilitates the sort of informal, more spontaneous get-togethers that seem to better suit adult bereaved siblings' life circumstances eg work, children and studies.

A common theme I've noticed is new members' sense of relief upon realising that a forum exists just for them. Often, joining the SIBBS Facebook group is the first chance bereaved siblings may have had to share their story and talk to others who instantly 'get it', without need for explanation or fear of judgement. Often they have been struggling alone for some time, years even, without feeling comfortable to share their pain. Getting those unbearable words out in a forum where they will be heard and understood can be immensely healing and help to relieve a bereaved sibling's burden.

2 Get Togethers
Informal get togethers are arranged up and down the country via Facebook. They give us the opportunity to share stories of our brother or sister with other bereaved siblings, where we may not feel comfortable or able to do so with regular friends, partners, family or colleagues. Exchanging stories with others is an important part of our journey of grief.

It's also just comforting to share space and a drink with familiar, kindred spirits who know where you're at emotionally. The friendships that form between bereaved siblings occupy a special place, no more or less important, but certainly distinct from other everyday and longstanding friendships.

3 Our Newsletter
Our regular SIBBS newsletter, in digital format, is another way siblings can share their stories and remember and honour their brothers and sisters. We also use the newsletter to cover mental health issues that coincide with grieving.

It is a place to share what helps us cope in our grief - for instance a SIBBS member recently shared how journaling has helped her - and to celebrate inspiring art and cultural projects related to grief and loss.

***

SIBLING RETREATS
by Rachael Claye
Once or twice a year, TCF holds a retreat for adult bereaved siblings. The numbers have crept up each year, and for good reason. As bereaved siblings we deal not only with our sadness,

but the loneliness of losing a comrade who shared our childhood, who was present in our development towards adulthood, and who we expected to be there until the end. When they die, our family changes shape forever; so do our parents; so do we.

It is always incredibly hard for people arriving at a retreat for the first time. It was for me. I'd asked TCF if we could hold a one-off retreat for siblings after running into others like me at a TCF National Gathering. There were only a few of us survivor children, but still it felt like a healing balm to be alone in a room together. I thought how comforting it would be to have a gathering just for us.

TCF kindly agreed, and helped to fund it. And sure enough, it was gut-wrenching to turn up that first time, just fifteen of us. But very quickly the fellow feeling and understanding changed the atmosphere in the room. I think all of us left that first weekend retreat for siblings having shared a lot of tears but also some laughter. You only see the humour when you open up with others who know exactly what you're talking about.

Since then our retreats have grown in size and frequency. It's often hard for adult siblings, who generally have jobs and caring responsibilities, and are often also trying so hard to support grieving parents, to find time for their own grief. The retreat provides that. From Saturday lunchtime to Sunday afternoon, we are all of us in it together.

EXHAUSTION

'I am not an early bird or a night owl.
I am some form of permanently exhausted pigeon.'
Lorraine Lynn

I found that even the simplest tasks were hard to do. I had to remind myself to eat. But what was I to eat? The effort to think about meals and then to shop for them was too great. Robin died in March and the spring that year was very warm. I sat in the garden under the apple tree in the dappled shade all day. The thought of what I had to do next was too exhausting.

And as for housework. Forget it. What was the point. And anyway I was too exhausted. But I could manage to pick up my pen and jot down:

> 'So what if your house is a mess.
> Leave it. Tomorrow you just might
> need to wring hell out of a dishcloth
> or beat up a rug or two.'

I met a lovely bereaved Dad, Peter Campbell, at one of our residential weekends and what he said about normal everyday tasks now sapping our energy, made a good deal of sense.

UNWIRED!
by Peter Campbell
In our everyday lives a lot of thought processes occur without us realising. *On a 'normal' day our brains take over a variety of tasks without us thinking about them. This is referred to as being 'subconsciously competent'. We make tea, cook dinner, go shopping etc…*

But… when we experience the trauma of something so major, it invariably changes everything… our life, our thoughts, our hopes…

Our complex brains can 'unwire' themselves for a period of time and we can find ourselves, without being aware, thinking about every task we do. This is referred to as being 'consciously competent'. Everyday tasks sap our energy levels immensely, hence the reason why we feel so physically exhausted every day.

Knowing WHY we feel like this can be a huge step in the healing process.

***

Like most of us I wasn't aware of this at the time. I don't know whether I would have managed to take it all in, but I think if someone had said to me, 'It's normal to be unable to think clearly or do everyday tasks at the moment. You've had a traumatic shock and your senses and brain will take time to adjust. But slowly they will…' I think it would have really helped. I agree with Peter; knowing why we feel like this can be a huge step in the healing process.

OTHER ADVICE I WAS GIVEN:
Be easy on yourself. Grieving is hard work. Exhaustion is a common response. Try to get extra rest and take breaks. - For me, the extra rest wasn't a problem, I could hardly get out of bed in the morning.

Nourish your body. Take the time to eat in a healthy way. Even when not hungry try to eat small meals. - Far too full of common sense to be heeded at the time. My response to this was the following:

'………………..Order a pizza
or heat up one of the unknown
objects lurking in the freezer.
Hug a bowl of custard, have tomatoes
on toast for breakfast, lunch and tea,
Don't let them tell you how to grieve.'

My hair must have felt exhausted too as it started to come out on each side. I've now had it cut so that the rest of my hair falls forward so you can't tell. Strangely enough I rather like this style.

'You look sad today'
'Hm... I'm sad every day
I just didn't have the energy to hide it today'

Ask friends to understand that your appearance of 'doing well' may be deceptive because on the inside you're hurting badly. Grief is painful, it is tricky, and it is exhausting.

I want to share the following poem with you because it makes me smile.

If the mountain seems too big today
*then climb a hill instead
if the morning brings you sadness
it's ok to stay in bed
if the day ahead weighs heavy
and your plans feel like a curse
there's no shame in rearranging
don't make yourself feel worse
if a shower stings like needles
and a bath feels like you'll drown
if you haven't washed your hair for days
don't throw away your crown
a day is not a lifetime*

a rest is not defeat
don't think of it as failure
just a quiet, kind retreat
it's ok to take a moment
from an anxious, fractured mind
the world will not stop turning
while you get realigned
the mountain will still be there
when you want to try again
you can climb it in your own time
just love yourself till then

Laura Ding-Edwards

It is so important, whatever you do, to be kind to yourself, to be gentle with yourself. You're exhausted and that's ok; you're grieving and that's exhausting. **However you're feeling, that's part of grieving.** And we all need to let ourselves grieve.

'Whatever you're doing, love yourself for doing it.'

BREATHING

'Breathing isn't a big step in the grief process, but it is the most important one.'

BREATHING

Have you noticed that when you are grieving, your breathing can be very shallow, or that you are holding your breath without even realising it? This is not abnormal in grieving. Grief affects every part of us, including our breathing. I jotted down the following:

> I must be gentle with myself
> at this time,
> Not beat myself up thinking of
> things not done.
>
> For it takes endless patience
> to grieve,
> And all my energy today
> just to breathe.

I found I was giving great sighs every now and again. It took me some time to realise why I was doing this. When I sighed deeply I was taking in much needed air because I was breathing in such a shallow way. It really helped me to know why I was feeling out of breath and that it was normal.

The more you notice how you feel, what your thoughts are, how your body is affected by your responses to the world around you, the less out of control you can begin to feel.

But don't take a huge breath into your chest; breathing deeply is about taking a slow breath into your stomach. Apparently this helps to get more oxygen into the brain and so to decrease anxiety. - I'm starting to do this now as I'm writing this. I'm very suggestible…

Have a go at the following…

A BREATH OF SUMMER - ANYTIME
by Darcie Sims

When we are hurting or in a hurry or under great stress, we grab at the air, pulling it in as fast as we can. We swallow great gulps of air, inhaling and exhaling as quickly as possible. We never really quite fill our lungs because we are gasping at the air. We are almost desperate in our attempt to breathe.

Breathing isn't a big step in the grief process, but it is the most important one! *Without breathing, nothing else works. And since we are breathing, we might as well enjoy its healing capabilities.*

So, as you sit on the step, or lie down in the grass, begin to become aware of your breathing. Notice how and when you take in air and how and when you release it. Do you grasp at the air, grabbing at the air, trying to fill your lungs to capacity? Or do you merely 'sip' at the air, allowing small amounts to slip past your lips? Perhaps breathing deeply hurts in some way, causing muscle spasms or memories to flood across your mind…

Become aware of your breathing and try to orchestrate your breath. Bring air in through your nose, holding it for a count of 1-2-3 and then let it escape past your lips. Inhale through your nose and exhale through your mouth. Feel your breath and follow it as it flows through your body. Breathe in through your nose, imagining the oxygen flowing through every cell in your body, bringing its healing energy to every corner of yourself. Exhale through your lips, letting the used-up air rise all the way up from your toes; and send it out of your body, letting it escape through your mouth.

You can even add sounds to the breathing out, if you wish. Listen to your body and find the sounds that may be hiding somewhere within you. You can find those sounds and let them go as you release your breath. Perhaps you find a groan or some anger that needs expressing. Perhaps it is a song or laughter that bubbles up and out. Whatever the sounds, let them come, as you allow your breath to be released.

You may find tears coming as you practice this breathing technique. Let them come as well as any feelings that rise to your awareness.

> ***Healing begins when feelings are recognised, acknowledged, and released.***

As you continue to breathe in through your nose and out through your mouth, you might wish to close your eyes and let your mind begin to drift. Grow quiet and find the rhythm of your body, breathing in a way that feels comfortable to you. Perhaps you can imagine a warm light shining down on the top of your head. It is just like sunlight dancing across your forehead, warming your whole being.

As you continue breathing, imagine that sunlight moving down your body, drifting slowly across each part of your body. Imagine the sunlight caressing the back of your neck and your shoulders, easing away the tension that we often carry there.

Imagine the sunlight flowing down your shoulders, your elbows, across your chest. As the warmth of this summer sun washes across your body, you can feel the tension leaving. The cares of the winter drift down your legs and leave through your toes. You feel lighter, softer, calmer.

As you begin to feel more at peace, let your imagination create a 'safe place' for you. *Find a summertime memory* that brings feelings of warmth, safety, and pleasure to you. You might find yourself on the beach, feeling, seeing, hearing the waves wash across the sand. You might be standing in a mountain meadow, surrounded with wild flowers, the sounds of a gentle mountain stream calling you to rest.

Whatever picture comes to you as you spend a few moments in reflective breathing, enjoy it completely. Smell the smells of your favourite place. Taste the tastes, hear the sounds of this magical moment. It is yours, deep within you, a place of safety and calmness.

You can find this quiet within anytime you need to, just by becoming aware of your breathing, always breathing in through your nose and exhaling through your mouth. As you become more experienced in this breathing technique, you will find you can create any scene you wish, creating any landscape you find comforting. You can create a summertime place anywhere, any time. You just have to breathe and imagine.

- Breathe in peace. Exhale tension. Let it go out of you, imagining our summertime sun warming each part of your body.

- Breathe in joy. Exhale sadness. Blow out the grief, if only for a single moment. Feel your heart becoming lighter, your pain growing less.

- Breathe in love. Exhale grief. Let the light of your loved one's life fill you with memories, not just of summer time, but of every time you laughed and sang and danced and dreamed and loved.

Make the commitment to grow quiet within and listen to the music of yourself. Take one small footstep each day. Make one small change each day. It only takes a moment to find the magic *within. So, here in the warmth of summertime, find the peace that is deep within you and let it bring comfort to yourself and others. Be gentle in your despair and trust the wisdom within.*

Find a new wholeness for yourself this summer. Find the balance of heart and mind that allow the memories to heal rather than hurt. Come out of hiding in the summertime and let the breath of summer begin to heal the hurts. Breathe in love and find the memories and the magic of those who have loved us. Love is the magic that heals us all.

***

As time has gone by I still feel being aware of how I'm breathing is very important. Sometimes when I'm rushing around, trying to do all the things on my list, and beginning to feel exhausted, I stop and remind myself to breathe slowly and more deeply, instead of just snatching breaths to keep going.

What I find is this: the slower, deeper breathing calms and relaxes me. I still carry on with the things I have to do, but I find I'm getting them done more easily, and can carry on for longer, so that by the end of the day I can pour myself a glass of red wine, put my feet up, and instead of beating myself up about what I haven't done, pat myself on the back for the things I have managed to do.

Try it…

DREAMS

Do you dream about your child, grandchild or sibling?
Only rarely have I dreamt about Robin and Nikki. Part of
me wishes I could drift off to sleep and be with them again
but part of me thinks, 'No, I don't want that raw feeling of
horrendous loss to descend on me when I wake the following
morning.'

THE MYSTERY OF DREAMS
by Margaret O'Neill, Edinburgh, April 2003
*I seldom dream about Hugh since his death. This surprises me.
Physically, we were very close; he often crept into our bed in
the night or in the early morning to put off going to school.
So when the mother of one of his classmates dropped off a hot
meal for us one afternoon shortly after he had died and asked,
'Have you dreamt about Hugh?', I reluctantly replied, 'No'. She
expressed some surprise at my response. 'Oh! if it was me, I'd
be dreaming about him every night'.*

*Now apart from the anger and hurt this response caused me,
it also touched a question that I'd been asking myself then and
still do now. 'Why don't I dream about Hugh?' Like my visitor,
I imagined that because of the closeness of the bond between
Hugh and me, and because he was - and is - so much a part of
my conscious life, naturally, he would be very much a part of
my dream life.*

*Not so. On the two or three occasions I have dreamt about him,
I have been unable to communicate with him. In one dream
he was lining up in the school playground. When I realised
he was there at the end of the line I called to him. I wanted
to ask him where he'd been, tell him how happy I was to see
him. Surprisingly, Hugh didn't want to speak to me. He was*

reluctant to involve me in what he was doing and there was a great sense of independence about him. I felt confused and disappointed by the apparent rejection.

More recently, as I've tried to understand and make sense of this unfamiliar distance and separation in our relationship, I've been reminded of a biblical scene depicted by many great artists, including Titian, Holbein, Brueghel and others. The subject is often given the title, 'Noli me Tangere' - translated as 'do not touch'. These are the words spoken to Mary Magdalene by Jesus when he appears to her after the resurrection. In her happiness at seeing her 'rabboni' or 'teacher' whom she loves, she reaches out to hold him.

Uncharacteristically Jesus puts up his hand and commands her, 'Noli me tangere', 'do not touch me' or 'do not cling to me - do not hold on to the relationship we once had'. He indicates to Mary that his death has changed their relationship but that there is a new one to come, something not yet realised and unfamiliar.

I find this imagery quite helpful in trying to interpret my dreams of Hugh. I desperately miss and ache for the physicality and familiarity of our relationship but it gives me a sense that there is more to come.

Nowadays, I don't fret that I haven't dreamt about Hugh. The lack of dreams doesn't mean I've forgotten about him or that our relationship has ended. Rather, that my love for him continues in a different way. His death may have changed our relationship, but it hasn't ended it. Taking one small step towards something new is a real sign of hope in our lives and extends our relationship with them. Our child has meaning for us in the things we do now, not just in the things we used to do for them.

***

ALTHOUGH I HAVE RARELY DREAMT about Robin and Nikki, there was one 'dream' that affected me deeply. Not long after Nikki died, I was lying in bed one morning, when I saw her standing at the bottom of my bed.

She was smiling and looking at me, and said, 'I'm fine, Mum, I'm okay'.

I told myself it must have been a dream, but it was like no other dream I've ever had. It felt so real. The whole incident brought me great comfort and still does.

I shared this dream with my friend, Mary, and she shared the following with me:

MY DREAM
by Mary Hartley

I also had a very vivid dream, which I'm almost a hundred per cent sure wasn't a dream at all. It happened in 2008, when my daughter, Karen, was pregnant for the first time. We went to see King Lear at the Globe and, of course, all of his daughters die and that night I dreamed Karen had died.

I texted her the next morning to make sure it wasn't real and then I was just sitting up in bed thinking that it could happen, there are no guarantees, and I was so miserable. Then I looked up and there was Claire and she was lit up with happiness.

She was telling me that, no matter what happens here on earth, it's all going to be ok in the end and we'll all be together again. I said, 'Claire is this really happening?' and she said she'd prove it to me by blowing on my arm and, sure enough, I felt something blow gently up and down my arm. I couldn't see her any more then but I sensed her presence for a few days afterwards. It was a very strange but very positive experience.

I also had some lovely dreams, of Claire and my mum, in the weeks after my mum died. Losing a parent isn't the same as losing a child, of course, but it was hard because mum had been my rock, my confidant, my saviour almost, after Claire died and she knew, better than anyone, how deeply I was grieving, how much I missed my daughter and how much I worried in case she was unhappy and frightened because I couldn't be there for her anymore.

Thinking back to those dreams, is making me smile because they were joyous. The pair of them were always together, were always happy and laughing and were having a great time, and quite often up to no good. In one of them, for example, they were in a big posh department store skating across the floor, knocking rails of dresses over, shouting 'wheeeee' and laughing and laughing. They were both 'party animals', my mother and my daughter, and I love to think of them like this.

I often wonder whether my dreams were a result of my grief stricken brain, trying to make sense of things, or was my mum reassuring me and letting me know my Claire was ok? I rather like to think it's the latter.

DREAMING OF EMILY
by Sharon Rose
I very rarely dream, and if I do, I hardly ever remember my dreams. I keep my iPad by my bed so that I can watch TV or look things up when I can't sleep, so I've got into the habit of writing down my dreams.

Emily used to dream vividly all the time and kept post-it notes by her bed to write them down. They were often about herself with characters from TV programmes or friends from school but fully formed and beautifully written.

I know that I've woken up in tears a couple of times when I've been holding on tightly to Emily in a dream and she leaves me. Or if I've had an argument with her - I remember clearly telling her that she wasn't allowed to go out as I knew she'd be dead if she went.

But there was one dream recently where I woke up so happy, as she was cuddling me and letting me stroke her. She was 11 or 12 in the dream and she was laughing and playing with her best friend. We were having a party with friends at home in the garden and it was a hot summer's day. I remember that the dream lasted for ages and so did the happy feelings.

I wonder if we could train ourselves to dream positively and then maybe we'd always wake up with a smile.

***

OH, WHAT A GREAT IDEA, SHARON! I'd love to be able to train myself to dream positively. Just think of it; if we went to bed each night knowing we were going to have a dream that would lift our spirits, then hopefully we would be able to get through the day in a far better mood, even tackle the washing up with gusto… But of course, that's just a dream…

NEAR DEATH EXPERIENCES (NDEs)

I did not know much about Near Death Experiences before I looked them up on the internet. Thinking back though, I do remember a friend of mine who is a Roman Catholic priest, telling us that he thought of death as a second birth. Just as a baby in the womb, as it is struggling through the dark birth canal, has no idea of the light of the world into which it will be born, we too have no idea of the possible world into which we are to die. This idea is put very clearly by Kenneth Ring PhD:

THE GREATEST GIFT
by Kenneth Ring PhD
When we are born, we emerge out of the constriction of the womb and birth canal into the wondrous world of previously unimaginable and virtually unlimited sensory experience. And when we die, we go through a second birth, which may be even more difficult than the first, leave the world we know for another that transcends anything we can conceive where we discover, finally, what it is to be alive. 'Fully alive, and filled with a radiant joy, beyond the realm of happiness.' This is the the message those who have made the journey, but survived, have to tell those who are about to undertake it. It is the greatest gift that they have to share.

NEAR DEATH EXPERIENCES
by Mary Hartley
Near Death Experiences were first written about in 1975 by an American doctor called Raymond Moody in the ground-breaking book, 'Life After Life'. People who had come close to death, from illnesses, accidents or cardiac arrest for example, reported feelings of great peace and calm, of leaving their bodies

and of being drawn through a long white tunnel into a wonderful light where they would often meet with relatives and friends who had died, and would feel wrapped in love.

For a few years there was a fair amount of scepticism about these claims but, as the years have gone by, more and more NDEs have been reported and there have now been hundreds of thousands from every continent and almost every country across the globe.

Nowadays most doctors and scientists accept these experiences are real, although there is disagreement about the cause. Clinicians have tried to prove that they are caused by low oxygen levels in the blood or by too much morphine, for example, but none of the explanations suggested so far have fitted with the experiences people are having.

So that leaves us with the rather intriguing thought that there might not be a logical physical reason for NDEs but maybe they are exactly what they seem to be; a window into a life after this life. Experiments into the phenomena are being conducted in several countries at the moment and many very interesting books have been written on the subject.

In the UK a nurse called Dr Penny Sartori PhD, RGN was commissioned by the NHS to conduct a five year investigation into NDEs because, whatever the reason for them, they can have a significant effect on patients. Her books, 'The Wisdom of Near-Death-Experiences' and 'The Transformative Power of Near-Death Experiences', are well worth reading as are many others on the same subject.

I've been fascinated by NDEs since I read Raymond Moody's first book in 1975 and now, as a bereaved mother who was present in the room during her daughter's cardiac arrest, unsuccessful resuscitation attempt and subsequent death, they bring me comfort and hope.

KEEPING GOING

Right, I'm up. Ok, still in my dressing gown, but you have to start somewhere… Now, what am I going to do today. There is lots to be done, so I'd better 'seize the day…'

Carpe Diem - Sieze the Day

A new day is an opportunity not to be missed
I must make a list.

There are so many things to be done;
first, I'll put the kettle back on.

I need another cup of tea
just of course for energy.

Next, there's that last piece of blackberry tart
then I really will make a start.

It's not that I'm lazy or slacking,
deep down I want to get cracking.

I'll get round to things soon
and seize the afternoon.

Gina Claye, from *Don't Let Them Tell You How to Grieve*

I wonder what I would be doing if I still had my Nikki and Robin… Life would be so different… I could be getting on a plane, going out to visit Robin in Singapore, sitting in the garden with Nikki, chatting, even perhaps planning a wedding…

Right, I can sit here dwelling on what would have been, carry on wishing they were still here… I can hear Rob's voice in my head, 'Mum get up and do something; get up and put the kettle on… again.'

I come to with a start. I can carry on like this all morning, just slipping into the past, wishing, not really being aware I'm doing it.

What was I doing…? I was making another list. Right, I'll start again.

Eat breakfast
Get dressed
Shopping
Come back and have a coffee
Remember Nikki and Robin while I'm drinking my coffee
Best to put aside a time to remember them

That's enough for now. I suppose I'd better get on with it. Wonder if I've got any clean socks…

What I find works is this: when I've completed something on my list I put a smiley face next to it. If I don't manage to do it I put an arrow meaning, 'get it done tomorrow'.

If I've already done something which I've forgotten to put on my list, I write it down and immediately add a smiley face - that gives me a fantastic lift.

I came across this poem in an old TCF Newsletter and had to smile.

Resignation

I am hereby tendering my resignation as an adult.
I have decided I would like to accept the responsibilities
*   of an 8 year-old again.*
I want to go to McDonald's thinking it's a four star
*   restaurant.*
I want to sail sticks across a fresh mud puddle and make
*   a pavement with stones.*

I want to think Smarties are better than money because
* you can eat them.*
I want to lie under a big oak tree and run a lemonade
* stall with my friends*
on a hot summer's day.

I want to return to a time when life was simple;
When all you knew were colours, multiplication tables,
and nursery rhymes, but that didn't bother you,
because you didn't know what you didn't know and you
* didn't care*
All you knew was to be happy because you were blissfully
* unaware*
of all the things that should make you worried or upset.

I want to think the world is fair.
That everyone is honest and good.
I want to believe that anything is possible.
I want to be oblivious to the complexities of life and be
overly excited by little things again.

I want to live simply again.
I don't want my day to consist of computer crashes,
mountains of paperwork, depressing news,
how to survive more days in the month
than there is money in the bank, mortgages, gossip,
* illness,*
And, most of all,
The loss of loved ones.

I want to believe in the power of smiles, hugs, a kind
* word,*
truth, justice, peace, dreams, the imagination, mankind,
and making angels in the snow.

*So... here are my chequebook and car-keys, my credit
  cards
and my pension statements.
I am officially resigning from adulthood.*

*If you want to discuss this
further,
you'll have to catch me first,
because...*

Thanks to the unknown author

Don't we all feel like that sometimes; we want to run
away from 'all this'. I used to take life for granted. I didn't
appreciate fully how much I had in what I thought was just a
very ordinary life. If I was going to carry on and live any kind
of meaningful life after such devastating loss I was going to
have to dig deep and keep on going.

REACHING DEEP
**In his book 'When Life Hurts: A Personal Journey from
Adversity to Renewal', Rabbi Wayne Dosick tells this story
about the world-renowned violinist, Itzhak Perlman.**
*Childhood polio left Perlman able to walk only with the aid
of two crutches and with braces on both of his legs. When he
plays a concert the journey from the wings to centre stage is
slow and laborious. Yet, once he begins playing, his incredible
talent transcends any thought of physical challenge.*

*One evening, Perlman was scheduled to play a most difficult
violin concerto at one of the world's most famous recital
halls. He slowly made his way on stage, set aside his crutches,
unloosed his leg braces, took up his violin and nodded to the
conductor to begin.*

Only a few bars into the concerto one of the strings on Perlman's violin broke with a rifle-like popping noise that filled the entire auditorium. The orchestra immediately stopped playing, and the audience held its collective breath. Most assumed that Perlman would have to put on his braces, take up his crutches and slowly walk off stage to get a new string. Or, perhaps. an assistant would come out with a new string or a substitute violin.

But, after just a moment's pause, Perlman set his violin under his chin, and signalled to the conductor to begin again.

An eyewitness recounted, 'Now I know that it is impossible to play a violin concerto with just three strings. I know that, but that night Itzhak Perlman refused to know that. You could see him modulating, changing, and recomposing in his head. At one point it sounded as if he were retuning the strings to get new sounds from them that they had never made before.

'When he finished there was an awesome silence in the room. And then people rose and cheered - we were all on our feet, screaming and cheering. He smiled, wiped his brow, raised his bow to quiet us and then he said, not boastfully, but in a quiet pensive tone: "You know, sometimes it is the artist's task to find out how much music you can still make with what you have left".'

***

I'm going to carry that phrase with me each day, 'It is the artist's task to find out how much music you can still make with what you have left'. Only I'm going to change it slightly and say to myself each day:

'It is my task to find out how much difference I can still make with what I have left.'

UKO

- Upright with Knickers On -

I didn't want to get up in the morning! I bet you didn't too. I didn't want to wake up! I didn't want to have to go through the realisation again that Nikki was dead. But I couldn't do anything about that, I couldn't change the past; now I had to get through the day somehow.

I had to get the other children off to school. That gave me one reason to get up. I have friends who have lost their only child and I can't begin to imagine what that is like. All I know is that, somehow, after the prostrating grief of the early years, these wonderful people have found a reason to live again and are making a difference to the lives of others.

OK, I'm up and of course, had my cup of tea, now what am I going to do with the rest of my day?

WHAT I DO TO HELP MYSELF
by Tricia Swaby
Our 23 year old son, Daniel, ended his life in 2001. I received a lot of support and comfort from my church. Many of the congregation were either Irish or of Irish extraction and they could talk very freely about death in the way others find hard.

I read up on suicide to try to fathom out what happened and I joined the Compassionate Friends and Papyrus. Margaret Brunskill, who was involved in both organisations, was a great comfort as she had had a similar experience. I will always be grateful to her.

I found practical crafts useful such as sewing patchwork, dressmaking and knitting, especially on dark winter nights. In summer I worked in the garden.

We set up an award at Daniel's former Primary and Secondary schools for the child in their final year who has made the most effort, and it continues to this day.

Where I live there is lovely, hilly countryside so walking is always a nice way to relax.

I was still working and I was told at the time by a colleague that, 'the aggro at work will take your mind off it', and it did!

I go every week to the cemetery; one time there was an elderly man at a nearby grave visiting his wife's grave. He was cheerful and warm hearted and he was a comfort to me.

I still find birthdays are the hardest time. We have a special meal for Daniel's birthday and we take flowers, a birthday card and a lantern to the cemetery. Keeping the grave nice is a comfort as well.

After I retired I have kept myself busy with voluntary work - working in a charity shop, involvement with our local U3A and church and assisting 11 year olds who have problems with reading. I really do think that keeping socially and physically active is very important.

KEEPING GOING
by Joy Rooke

When Debbie died, I had so much to do with regard to her funeral, paperwork, notifying people and making sure her memory was kept alive... Then it was back to thinking about the pre-school I run and managing that again. I put Debbie 'away' somehow and carried on.

Then I found other people who had lost a child that I could talk to. This wasn't easy, but eventually through other people and God incidents (I am a committed Christian) bereaved parents came to me, and basically we helped each other and cried together too.

I retired early and started my Bereaved Parents Support group. I knew God wanted me to do this and that Debbie would expect nothing less of me. Now the group in Westcliff, Essex has gone from strength to strength and is a very close supportive group, with two sessions on a Monday once a month and a more casual meet up once a month at a local café overlooking the sea. I now feel a deep love and empathy for bereaved parents. This wouldn't have been possible before I lost my beautiful Debbie.

WHAT HELPS ME GET OUT OF BED
by Pauline Bevan

My daughter, Katie Button, died quickly and unexpectedly aged 36 of Meningitis W. on December 17th 2016. There are many things that help to get me out of bed since she died:

My responsibility to and love for others My remaining daughter and two grandchildren, doing my best to help them with their grief; they have lost a sister, an aunty. I do not want to inflict further pain or distress upon them. Their love for me supports me.

My cats, they need my care. My colleagues, they depend on me to turn up for work.

My belief, faith, hope and trust in God. I WILL see Katie again - what will I be able to tell her I have done to make her short life count.

God's love, support and guidance - of which I see the Compassionate Friends as being part. Knowing others are surviving this grief and that I am not alone.

My love for Katie: *To make her life count through me; I try to do good in her name, from small acts of kindness to some volunteer charity work. For example, picking up a piece of rubbish from the street and putting it in the bin, offering to help someone carry a bag to their car, smiling kindly at others, letting people out of junctions whilst driving, not rushing to get away when someone has started a conversation with me - giving more of myself to others. I also do bucket collections for charity when I can.*

When I do these things I say in my head, 'This is for you Katie'. With the bucket collections I tell the organisers why and in whose name I am doing it. I do these things to honour Katie. She did so much for charity and animal welfare.

These things are mostly successful in getting me out of bed each morning. However, as I know you will be only too aware, sometimes the sheer pain and heartbreak are so all consuming that nothing will work. Thankfully I have only had a few days since Katie died that I have not got out of bed or have had to go back to bed and just curl up, cry, give in. These days are so so horrible but I believe necessary, so in a way they also get me through.

WHAT HELPS ME
by Christina Ford
My son Adam died at 19. Three months after he died I set up an online memorial tribute site with Muchloved.com and that really helped me to write down my thoughts for several years. I received many thoughts and prayers from unknown people all over the world who had read his tribute and been touched by it. These thoughts, and candles lit for him by people we will never meet, have given me such comfort over the years and have often brought tears to my eyes.

I left my job as senior management business support to re-train as a bespoke florist. This started because, like so many of us, I was taking fresh flowers to Adam's grave each week and it's almost as if he was pushing me in a new direction, working with beautiful flowers, foliage and nature in general. I have now had my own designer floristry business www.saffronroseflowers.com for the last seven years and specialise in wedding floristry - celebrating life and new beginnings. I also teach floristry workshops.

For the last three years I have been doing classes in Iyengar yoga which is not the easiest of yoga practices but it focuses the breath, the mind and the body. It has helped in many ways, particularly focussing on the here and now i.e. not dwelling on the past or being anxious about the future. Dealing with 'now' focusses the mind and calms both mind and body.

My husband and I moved from the London suburbs to the Kent coast. Walking by the sea each day brings comfort, peace and calm - even though my son died by drowning. How this is I don't know but I don't question it.

I became a TCF group leader and local contact several years ago - hugely rewarding when you see bereaved families being able to open up and share their grief with others and to have hope where there was none. I know I have made a difference and that to me is a gift that I have been given and can pass on.

SOME THOUGHTS ON GETTING THROUGH MY GRIEF
by Marie Best

I lost Claire on the 12th June 2000; this was the day my world changed forever and my life as I knew it, ended. I was never to be the same again. How did I get through? What helped me? Where do I begin? The news was delivered by a policeman, I fled into the garden, not allowing him to complete his sentence. 'Your daughter —.'

How did I get through the frenzied grief of the early days, waking up to the confusion of the early morning, writing letters, searching through belongings, feeling blown apart, scattered, not knowing how I would function in the world, a world of sunshine, rain and seasons changing? I hated spring, the beauty of the autumn colours made me sad, the darkness of winter was hard and then - Christmas and the new year! I remember these words going round in my head...'Stop the world, I want to get off'.

I read a lot; I wrote my thoughts down each evening, expressing my confusion, longings, sorrow, pain and anguish. I cried on to each page. I went back to work, I felt I had to as I had started this new job five weeks before. Retrospectively, work gave me a structure and I was possessed by a 'manic energy' that drove me forward. I had some counselling prior to the Inquest and was able to pour out my intense emotions without feeling judged. It helped to speak confidentially to an independent person. I knew nothing was going to 'fix' me, or put me together again. Just like Humpty Dumpty; this was just not going to happen.

I joined The Compassionate Friends and Papyrus; both organisations formed by bereaved parents. I could express my grief, talk to other parents bereaved in the same way and be understood. I could talk about Claire. I could read and write about my grief. I had joined two clubs that no parent would wish to join.

*Attending my first Papyrus meeting helped. I was doing something important; helping to prevent further young suicides. I was not an 'alien'. I was 'not singled out', others went there before me. It was a relief and comfort to know I was not alone, that my feelings and thoughts were shared. I was, along with others, taking action and addressing some of the issues I felt were **not** right with Claire's treatment. Now, 18* *years later, the problems surrounding mental health have at last come to the forefront. I felt and still feel that I was 'doing' something positive and contributing to changes in the mental health arena.*

My life, I realised, was irrevocably changed; but still I had a life that I had to live!! I began to discover how exhausting grief was and how important it was to take small steps, to rest, to be kind to myself, to understand that, at times the all-consuming guilt was not an absolute reality.

I started practising yoga again, with meditation. I found solace in quiet moments, in the beauty of the countryside. I travelled to India, where I was born, on a major birthday. This brought reconnection with my roots which was painful, but grounding. I continued to travel and visited Egypt. It marked the beginning of my 'before' and 'after' life. I was fascinated by the history, the temples and tomb art and their respect for death and the afterlife.

There was peace and calm in the desert, silence. It provided space, peace. I returned when the tourists were down in numbers and have repeated my visits almost annually. It was my escape to solace. I walked every morning in the gardens of the hotel, sat quietly with my thoughts. I felt a deep connection with the past. I felt like a broken old pot, like many buried in the desert sand. **I began to see that 'broken and old' could be mended and put together; brought back to life, changed, renewed and loved.**

My interest in Egyptology had left me, but recently, there has been a revival in my interest. I have started to explore again, visiting tombs, temples and museums; read and take guided tours. Claire, of course, travels with me.

***

WHAT HELPS ME 'GET THROUGH'
by Mandy Glass

I lost my son, Aiden, in 2015. At first of course, the pain was too raw to do anything but as my head cleared, I found that I could absorb myself in card making. I had been making cards before I lost Aiden, but only to send to family and friends on their birthdays. After losing Aiden, I found it occupied my mind a little but didn't require too much decision making. It was perfect for giving me something to focus on that wasn't too difficult. As each card is finished, you can admire what you have achieved and even if its all you have done that day, you have something to show for it.

I made so many that they were stacked up in the lounge. I decided I would sell them for charity, and had little stickers printed to put on each card saying, 'Made by Mandy Glass in memory of Aiden Platt'. I had been receiving a lot of help from Cruse Bereavement Care so I sold the cards and raised money for my local branch. I sold them in the Cruse office, in my workplace, and to family and friends. This way, I could carry on making lots more.

Then I discovered jigsaw puzzles! Jigsaw puzzles are great. You can get them in varying amounts of pieces depending on how good or bad you feel. I tend to buy mine from car boot sales or charity shops as they are a fraction of the price of new ones, then I give them to charity shops so raising more money. I find if I'm feeling ok, I can do 1000 piece puzzles but if I'm having a rougher time than usual, I go for 500 piece ones. They are great as they don't involve having to make decisions; you can just sit and place pieces where they should go. Once one is finished, you can admire it, then break it up and get excited about which one you will do next.

PLEASE DON'T

*'Next person that minimises my grief is getting a
swift kick to the shin.'*

**It's interesting what you can find on the internet, especially
on facebook pages.** Maria Ahern, besides giving much
excellent advice, frequently blows a gasket…

LISTENING
When I ask you to listen to me, please don't:

> *Start giving advice*
>
> *Try to 'solve my problem'*
>
> *Tell me I shouldn't feel this way*

*When you accept that I do feel what I feel, no matter how
irrational, then I can stop trying to convince you, and start to
understand what's behind this irrational feeling.*

So please listen to me and accept me, just as I am.

***'IF MY CHOICE IS BETWEEN GRIEVING MY BELOVED
CHILD'S DEATH IN THE WAY THAT WORKS BEST
FOR ME OR BEING YOUR FRIEND, YOU'RE GOING TO
LOSE…'***
*Saw this today and I was reminded that I am so blessed to
have amazing people in my life. The friends who are still with
me totally understand and acknowledge my grief. Luckily for
me, those that didn't want to face my pain, left quietly but they
are few and far between. And you know what? I can barely
remember who they were. Fight for your grief. Your child's
memory is contained within it and it's yours to keep… however
you wish to store it.*

I will not pretend to be okay for the sake of people who don't understand. My love and my loss are too big to hide, and it's not my job to make you feel better. Always remember this: It's never okay to criticise a grieving parent. EVER. You have no idea how hard it is to live without your child, and your inability to understand doesn't mean I'm doing it wrong.

It means you need to put that much more effort into loving and supporting me.

THAT PHRASE…!

Arghhhhh!!! If I hear that phrase one more time I might just blow a gasket! Luckily no one has said it to me… well not for a while anyway… But listen up world. It you tell a bereaved parent that it's 'TIME THEY MOVED ON', you're a twit of the highest order. I mean Trump style twit. Just imagine yourself leaving your child somewhere and walking away from them and not going back. No? Good. Hmmm… So why on earth do you think you have the right to tell us to do it.

Stop giving bereaved parents advice on what you think they should do. We have experts for that. You can just be a friend. If that's too uncomfortable, then maybe YOU can MOVE ON. If you are a friend, be supportive and don't ever tell a bereaved parent that it's time they did anything. Grief has no clock.

!!!

READING

I found it difficult to read books at first. I simply couldn't concentrate on page after page of words. I tended to dip into poetry. And I collected quotes. Quotes appealed to me because they got straight to the point. I stuck them on cupboard doors in the kitchen so that I could read them when I was doing chores - when I got round to them. Here are some of them:

> 'A strong person knows they have strength enough for their journey
> But a person of strength knows that it is in the journey where they will become strong.'
>
> **Nishan Panwar**

> 'They who are near me do not know
>   that you are nearer to me than they are,
> They who speak to me do not know
>   that my heart is full with your unspoken words,
> They who crowd in my path do not know
>   that I am walking alone with you,
> They who love me do not know
>   that their love brings you to my heart.'
>
> **Rabindranath Tagore**

'Look upon each day that comes as a challenge, as a test of courage. The pain will come in waves, some days worse than others, for no apparent reason. Accept the pain. Do not suppress it. Never attempt to hide grief from yourself. Little by little, just as the deaf, the blind, the handicapped develop with time an extra sense to balance disability, so the bereaved will find new strength, new vision, born of the very pain and loneliness which seem, at first, impossible to master.'

Daphne du Maurier

'If life throws lemons at you, stick them in the gin.'

Do you find reading about the experience of other bereaved parents helps you? As time passed and I was more able to concentrate, I read books about other bereaved parents' journeys through grief and it helped and comforted me; it was good to know I was not alone. Mary Hartley, our TCF librarian, tells us how much reading has helped her.

HOW READING HELPED ME
by Mary Hartley
From a very early age I've been one of life's bookworms. *I've read for pleasure, of course, but also for knowledge and support, and any unfamiliar event in my life has sent me to a library or a bookshop. I've always been able to find something in print to help me. So, when my daughter died and I was cast into a totally unfamiliar landscape, my natural instinct was to find out how other parents had coped with this most devastating loss and what I could do to help myself.*

Initially, for the first time ever, I couldn't find what I wanted. In those, for me, pre-Amazon days, I was reliant on my local library and bookshop and they let me down badly. However within a few months I found TCF and our amazing library and I was like someone dying of thirst in a desert who'd happened upon an oasis. I read books at the rate of two or three a week and they helped me so much.

Many of the books were written by bereaved parents and those that weren't were mostly based on the experience of bereaved parents. I read biographies, books of advice, anthologies, poetry, listened to audio tapes and suddenly I wasn't alone. There were so many people who'd lost their children; they'd walked in my shoes and they'd survived; there WAS hope for me. For years I had an emergency pile of books by my bedside and they got me through many a desperate 'wee small' hour.

Nowadays I manage the TCF library. I skim all our new books and read many of them and I can still feel that network of support they give me. Books remain my first port of call when I need advice about things such as my confused and chaotic emotions when I knew I'd be a grandmother for the first time, whether my terror every time my surviving daughter goes abroad is 'normal' or how other parents have marked their child's thirtieth birthday.

I'm committed to extending the network of support and hope, which our books can offer, to as many people as I can because I'm really not sure whether I could have survived without that.

***

Do join our TCF Library. When you first request books, Mary will chat with you to find out which would be the most appropriate books for you. She always encloses a letter in the parcel she sends…

(Details of TCF's library, The Catharine Pointer Memorial Library, and how to join can be found on our website at www. tcf.org.uk)

I didn't think of Audio Books at the time I was first bereaved. I listen to them a great deal now, especially in the car when I have a journey of many miles.

AUDIO BOOKS
by Mandy Howle
Audio books were a real lifeline for me. We live in rather an isolated place and in those days John worked away from home, so I was on my own for hours. The songs on the radio all seemed to be, 'I love you', 'I miss you,' etc. Classical music hurt too. I

just couldn't listen to music. So audio books helped me survive.

It is difficult to read when one is consumed by grief because all you can think about is the child that you long to see again. Concentration is poor. Audio books can also help during sleepless nights. You can hire them from the library and keep them out for three weeks; also nowadays you can get them on your iPad.

***

Back to my Quotes again

I have taken the first two lines of the next piece to heart and frequently say them to myself.

> *'It is a risk to attempt new beginnings.*
> *Yet the greater risk is for you to risk nothing.*
> *For there will be no further possibilities*
> *of learning and changing,*
> *of travelling upon the journey of life.*
> *You were strong to hold on,*
> *You will be stronger to go forward*
> *to new beginnings.'*
>
> **Earl Grollman** from *'Time Remembered'*

They remind me, if I'm feeling down, to try and keep positive… And if that fails I remind myself of another favourite of mine:

> *'If you feel you're about to go off the edge,*
> *Remember - the world is round!'*

WRITING

'Life is hard. I write words to make it softer.'

I write. As far as I can remember I've always scrawled down something or other. I remember writing a play for my friends to act when I was ten years old. I sat in the garage scribbling while they acted it out on the lawn. I've also written sketches and a one act play when I was part of a small amateur theatre group. It seems such a long time ago…

Perhaps you're imagining me now, writing this, sitting at my writing desk, everything organised. No…..

Where Do I Write?

Well…
Cooking… in the kitchen
making soup,
an idea simmers
I grab the indelible pen
and a scrap of paper from the drawer
Hastily jotting down words
while they're still stirring in my mind
splattering butter over the letters
while the onions splutter
and stick to the pan

Gardening…
Hacking back the weeds
an idea begins to germinate
In fear of forgetting
I rake round in my pocket
And with a stub of blunt pencil
plant it on a seed packet

Driving…
In the car coming home
I keep the words
wheeling round in my mind
until I can put on the brake
grab the biro
and on the back
of a long forgotten envelope
Release them.

As you can see, I'm not a bit disciplined about my writing…!

Grieving is doing, so that's what I did. I wrote a book called *Don't Let Them Tell You How to Grieve* just after Robin died. Having grieved for Nikki all those years ago I could recognise the various aspects of grief and it helped me enormously to write them down. I couldn't change what had happened, I couldn't control that but I could control the words - which ones to choose, what order to put them in. One of the poems I wrote for it was *The Photograph.*

The Photograph
At first I almost took the photograph
down. It showed the two of us
together, walking in the Chiltern hills.

We had stopped for a rest. I leant
against you, your arm round me,
my head on your shoulder.

The pain I felt each time I saw it
was so acute, it made me feel
again my overwhelming loss.

But to stare at the space it would
leave would be worse. So it
stayed. And gradually as time

passed, I made a friend of pain.
And now, in moments of anxiety,
I stand and look at the photograph.

I lean on you still and will all
my life. Your arm round me,
My head on your shoulder.

Writing 'lines' came naturally to me, so that's what I did. You might find other forms of writing come more readily to you, perhaps...

WRITING A GRIEF DIARY?

Getting it all down on paper can be a massive help, as Ann Wilkinson found out.

WHAT HELPED ME
by Ann Wilkinson

My elder son died 24 years ago aged 33. As you know, it seemed as if life stopped for the rest of us, but somehow we managed to keep going.

At the time I was teaching the violin in Dorset schools, and felt I just could not continue. My husband, a brass teacher in Southampton, felt it helped him to keep working doggedly on, day in and day out, so the first difference in our grieving surfaced immediately. We both went for counselling, and the counsellor suggested I should try writing my feelings down every day, a sort of grief diary, and it certainly helped me.

After a while, I decided to join a writing group, and I still belong to one. Now my writing is about many other subjects, and I no longer write about grief.

***

We may have a personal reason for writing a grief diary or we may simply want to fling words down to empty ourselves for the moment of feelings of anger, guilt, frustration, devastating loss, hopelessness and any other strong emotions.

Perhaps it can be described as a way of having an honest and open conversation with ourselves. Forget spelling, forget grammar too, you're writing only for yourself. You don't have to write in sentences either, just flinging down a rambling jungle of words will do. I've done this and found that some phrases I've looked at afterwards have started off a poem in my head.

Your journal is yours. Nobody need look at it. Just get pen and paper or computer and fingers and make a start. And perhaps… at a later time you can look back and see how far you've come…

I wrote down memories. I was terrified of forgetting things so I have a book where I just jot down memories as they cross my mind. I'm no writer so it is very much in note form but it's nice to look back at from time to time.

Liz Farmilo

WRITING A LETTER TO YOUR CHILD

Others I know have found writing a letter to their child has helped. You perhaps need no prompting on what to write but in case you want a little help, these are a few suggestions:

What things do I particularly remember about my child?
What do I miss most?
What do I need to explain?
What issues in our relationship remain unresolved?
What would I like to thank my child for?
What do I want to say sorry for?
What do I regret?

Is there anything I desperately need to say to my child?
What do I remember that made us both laugh?
How do I cope each day?
What do I hope for in the future?

HINTS TO GET YOU STARTED WRITING
If you've not had a go at writing before you might try this:
Choose **seven words** from out of a book or just out of your head and write **seven sentences.**

Perhaps you might choose these words, for example:
remember, last, thought, perhaps, ready, three, soon
Now put each word into a sentence:

Do you **remember**, my son,
The **last** time we were in the garden together
We **thought** we would plant a bed of wild flowers
Perhaps bees and butterflies would visit there
You were going to dig the soil, get it **ready**
I've dug it now, **three** days it took
It will **soon** be filled with wild flowers and memories of you.

I chose those seven words off the top of my head. I had no idea what I was going to write about. Once I had written the second sentence with the word last in and had chosen the word garden out of the air, my mind then, quite unexpectedly - or perhaps not - carried on with the garden theme and the other sentences followed on. Do try it, you might be surprised.

MICHAEL WILSON who has taken many Writing Workshops at our residential weekends has some helpful hints...

ON WRITING POETRY
by Michael Wilson

I began to write poems inspired by the loss of our daughter. I had no previous experience of writing poetry so I simply started to write conversations with my daughter as though she was still living.

I decided right from the start that I was going to avoid rhyming. The trouble with writing in rhyme is that you end up searching for rhyme rather than reason. A poem can end up as being doggerel and this is counter to feelings of profound loss.

When we've not written poetry before, non rhyming, free verse can be best for beginners who want to delve deeply into feelings. Free verse: line by line statements that hold together as poetry because of their depth of feeling and heightened means of expression and observation.

I recommend that you write lines of verse each beginning with a capital letter and let sentences start and finish where you think best, aiming for an intuitive, natural rhythmic feel to the words. A vivid recounting of memories will also encourage poetry as opposed to prose. Try always to be original and probably most important of all, use your five senses to increase intensity of observation. What sounds do you hear, what sights do you see, what things can you feel, what smells, what can you taste?

Here is an early poem I wrote. I hope it bears witness to some of the recommendations I make above.

Fragile Things
Fragile things have lasted years
Since you died:
Glasses, dishes, plastic spoons, whatever.
I can't understand their durability in the face of your loss.

Nor can I comprehend
The daffodils coming to life again,
Or my pond fish still here
When you are gone.

You were not fragile until you were fearless.
When the waters, rocks and stones
Showed how easy it was
To break you

Had you been more discerning,
Less careless, more caring of yourself,
You could still be here, washing these things -
Breaking them, not yourself.

Or looking out of this window
At the returning flowers of Spring.
Perhaps feeding the fish
That now rise to the surface again.

I think a lot about the moment
Your resolve would have broken
That instant when you said to yourself
'That's it, that's enough!' Or words to that effect.

That's how you would have gone,
I like to think:
No time to make a decisive break from
The world or consciousness or us?

What makes this poetry as opposed to prose? There is of course the actual shape of the words on the page, the use of capital letters at the beginning of each line; there is a rhythm here, the words sing along, and there is depth of observation - an intensity that is perhaps missing from prose. The other point to note is that a poem can be about anything, it doesn't have to be high and mighty.

The following poem, by Philippa Skinner, combines an annual event with deeply felt personal feelings:

Poppy Day
Remembering Jim, who died of a heroin overdose on November 7th, 2007

Misty morning,
Shrouded trees stand embarrassed
As, one by one, curled leaves
Drop to the dampening ground
Silently, reluctantly released.
And my heart lurches again
My darling, as the world loses light
And I remember.
Paper poppies sold anywhere
Worn carelessly
Call out everywhere
'It's that time again.'
(As if I needed reminding)
'To laud our heroes,
Lament their waste.'
And I remember
My young man -
Lived so harmlessly
Loved so powerfully
Felt so deeply
Cut down so callously
Wasted so needlessly
Died alone, so silently
Oh yes - I remember.

Died in a different war
But with no glory
And no hero's applause
Discounted, dismissed

No place in our history -
Except its shame -
And so I wear my poppy proudly
For you - because I remember.

Philippa Skinner

Another poem which illustrates much of what I have been trying to say about modern poetry is 'Making the Gravy' by Jill Yglesias (See chapter on Christmas) *It has a rhythm that changes according to what is being described, it has intensity of observation, it's not frightened of being emotive, it has great subtlety in the way it introduces tragedy to a simple domestic scene. And it doesn't waste words!*

I hope those of you who have not tried writing poems before - and of course those who have(!) will be encouraged to have a go at writing poetry yourselves. Free verse is very liberating and does not tie you to words merely because they rhyme. Every word in a poem can be significant, and perhaps one of the most important techniques is to go through your poem seeing which words you can leave out. Economy can be a good thing!

***

BLOGS

Or you might try writing a Blog. Maria Ahern has a regular conversation with her son, James, in our quarterly magazine, Compassion.

WEEK 188
by Maria Ahern

"What are you doing, ma?"

Thinking.

"Oh. That explains the funny face. What are you thinking

about so hard?"

I'm going to be speaking to a group of newly bereaved parents this evening, son, and I'm thinking about what I should say.

"Want some help?"

I think they do, yes.

"Not them...numpty! You! Do YOU want some help?"

Oh...yes son. Yes please.

"Ok. So Stephen Hawking can help too...Oi Steve, come over here a minute."

Are you actually with Stephen Hawking?

"No mum. Just teasing you. But he can actually help...he was a very clever man you know."

Yes, I kind of know that, James.

"So tell the parents this...'Remember to look up at the stars and not down at your feet...And however difficult life may seem, there is always something you can do and succeed at. It matters that you don't just give up.'"

Is that from you James?

"No. It's from Stephen."

Ok. It's a difficult concept though son. When there is so much pain that you can't see beyond it. Looking up and searching for answers. How do you find the answers?

"The answers to what?"

Well, the main question is, "Why?"

"*Hmmmm…Yes. I remember you screaming that, a lot, in the beginning.*"

So do I.

"*But what would you do with the answer, mum?*"

I don't know.

"*So there you go. It's a pointless question then, isn't it. As a lawyer you should know that it's pointless to ask a pointless question.*"

James, people whose lives have been destroyed don't think so logically.

"*I know, I know. But that's the point. In physical terms, what has happened is a total catastrophe. Of course it is. Now, standing still in the rabble and asking, 'Why', isn't going to provide any solace is it. Nor is it going to help. You must set about trying to adjust and rebuild. And, if possible, try and do it quickly before the storm breaks you completely. You must try and give the parents hope, mum. Tell them that while their life will never be the same, they have 'a life' and, while they do, with them, their children live on. So, looking down isn't helpful. Just tell them to look up.*"

Like in the piece we wrote a couple of years ago?

"*Yes, exactly like that…erm, I think it was mainly my work, but ok, I'll let you take the credit.*"

Thanks.

"*Anyway, back to our task. There's another bit of good advice from my new mate.*"

Joking?

*"Joking...but the advice is sound. It is simply this: **"For millions of years, mankind lived just like the animals. Then something happened which unleashed the power of our imagination. We learned to talk and we learned to listen. Speech has allowed the communication of ideas, enabling human beings to work together to build the impossible. Mankind's greatest achievements have come about by talking, and its greatest failures by not talking... All we need to do is make sure we keep talking."'***

Now that I can do!

"Don't we know it! So it's really very simple, mum. Just tell them to keep talking, and what seems impossible will become possible. See? You do it and you can help others do it too."

Oh James. I wish no-one ever had to learn to live in this state. I wish that there were no bereaved parents anywhere in the world and that my only job was to be your mummy.

"It's still one of your jobs, mum. Being a mummy doesn't end. But you have other jobs to do as well and you must keep on keeping on."

Ok son. I think I know what I'm going to say now. Thank you.

"You're welcome ma. Cool. Now I'm off to chat about the Big Bang theory..."

What!? You? Talking physics?

"No silly! The TV series...! See ya later ma. Hope your weekend goes well."

Thanks mate.

***

I look forward very much to reading Maria's blogs. They always make me laugh and there's a lot of wisdom in them. Michael Walford-Grant enjoys them too. He says:

'Maria Ahern's blogs entitled Week xxx, I find the most resonating I have ever read. They are so close to what it would be like if I was chatting with William.'

Michael Walford-Grant

ANNIVERSARIES

I know it's crazy, but as we approached the first anniversary of Nikki's death, I was convinced I could put the clock back… if only I knew how. I would tell myself I could get her some kind of treatment that would help her recover… I would stay with her all night… I would… my mind raced on and on. I would do things differently and it would be alright…

But of course it wasn't. The day arrived, March 25th, the day our Nikki had died - forever. After those few days of torturing myself I think I was glad it had actually arrived. What were we going to do? How were we going to remember her… to celebrate her? We needed to do something together, the whole family…

I don't know if you've ever played Pooh sticks… It's from the book, *Winnie-the-Pooh* by A A Milne. Pooh and friends drop a stick each on one side of the bridge then race over to the other side to see which one appears first.

Well we did the same thing with roses. On Nikki's first anniversary we took pink roses down to a small bridge over a nearby stream. We all had one rose each and dropped them at the same time from one side of the bridge and then raced over to the other side to see which one would appear first.

We watched them float down the winding stream, waving goodbye to them until they vanished out of sight. We then went to her grave and filled her vase with more beautiful pink roses, lit her candle,… stood around and stayed with her. The candle lit up her headstone:

> 'We are such stuff as dreams are made on
> And our little life is rounded with a sleep.'

In the evening we had a meal together, sitting round the table with her candle shining in the middle, trying, through our tears, to remember the good times…

When Robin died on March 18th 2003, we added yellow roses to the pink roses. As the two anniversaries were so close together, only seven days apart, we chose March 18th, which was Rob's anniversary and Nikki's birthday, to celebrate the lives of our two children.

Listen to this - Nikki died on 25th March. Robin died on Nikki's birthday, March 18th. His cat, Grobbelaar, died on his birthday, April 30th. My brother-in-law's birthday is also on April 30th and his dog died on April 30th too, the same day as Robin's cat. If I wrote this into a story the comment would probably be, 'highly unlikely'.

'We are not in control of many of the difficult - and traumatic - circumstances of our lives, but we are responsible for how we respond to them...
And I choose to honour their memory.'

Yesterday would have been Robin's 46th birthday. I don't need to tell you how I felt, as you will understand. Our children, grandchildren or siblings' anniversaries and birthdays come round each year and we cope with them as best we can.

I bought some lovely tulips of different colours and went to the grave and spent some time arranging them. I kept some of them to put in my sitting room. I'm looking at the vase now as I'm writing this. They are all standing upright with a slight sway as tulips tend to but two red ones are flopping right down. I've made sure they are in the water and tried to stand them up, but no good, there they are, flopped.

It made me sad at first but then I thought of Robin and what he would say, 'It's ok mum, leave them be, they've probably had a night out on the town,' and the thought made me laugh. I can hear him say, as he lay on the grass in the back garden looking at the clouds, 'Whatever dumps on you, Mum, you can always find something to bring you joy.' Remembering words of his like this always helps.

I hope that you remember things that your child or children, grandchild, brother or sister have said or done, and that this gives you heart. I hope also, that you find a way to celebrate their anniversaries as they come round each year - in the way YOU need to.

CELEBRATING CAMERON'S BIRTHDAY
by Kelly Cooper

I lost my son Cameron, my only child, to a cancerous brain tumour at the age of 13. This year will be Cameron's 21st Birthday. I always try to celebrate his birthday, not mourn it, as this is the day he came into my life. But as it was his 21st, I wanted to make it something special.

During Cameron's painful treatment he was advised to think of a 'happy place', somewhere where he had been happy, to reminisce about. He chose our holiday in Majorca and we spoke about it often.

Since his death I have returned to his 'happy place' each year, as this brings back happy memories, although tinged with sadness. So, this year, those close to Cameron will all embark on a week's retreat to Cameron's 'happy place' where we will raise a glass or two to celebrate his life and birthday.

However you 'celebrate' your child, grandchild or sibling's anniversary and birthday, may you remember all the happy memories and the love you shared, and take that with you into the following year.

MOTHER'S DAY

Whichever way I looked at it, this was not a day I wanted; another way of life sticking a knife in my back. I kept telling myself I was lucky, I still had a son and daughter. But I used to have two daughters and a son, and I no longer had Nikki, and the thought of Mother's Day rubbed it in.

So I had to do something. Sometimes the thought of a particular day is worse than the actual day itself. At least it's over in 24 hours. I bought a candle - where would we be without candles? - and decided I would celebrate the day I had become her mother and all the years she had been with me. The flame of the candle shone and became a real presence...

We walked and walked that day, came back and poured a glass of wine. I deserved it, and as midnight came round, I celebrated the fact that I had survived the day.

I still have the cards my son and daughter sent me, with their love and also with love from their sister. She remains with us all in our hearts.

I suspect we all have similar thoughts about Mother's Day!

I REMEMBER
by a Bereaved Mum
I remember vividly the first Mother's Day after my son died. Had there been a vote that year, I would have cast mine for the abolition of Mother's Day. I didn't want there to be such a day and I didn't want anybody to remind me that it did, indeed, exist. My response to those who were left who loved me was to pull away and isolate myself.

Between the first and second Mother's Day I made a number of discoveries. Probably the most important one I made was that my surviving child needed to be allowed to show her love for me. She was and is as important as my son who died and has that right. I also learned that my salvation lay in the hands of those people who cared for me, and when I learned to let them help me, I helped myself.

***

So, how do we cope with Mother's Day. Any ideas?

COPING WITH MOTHER'S DAY
by Sylvia Hornby
As to how I cope with the day… For Mothering Sunday I buy myself some flowers, as I can hear Christopher say, 'Buy yourself some flowers, Mum, from me and don't be sad'. I make a small arrangement with them around a candle and light it to burn throughout the day as a sign of his presence with me in my heart and mind. I am still Christopher's mother and always will be; it doesn't take a special day to remind me of the fact.

MOTHER'S DAY
On the one hand, I feel immense joy because I was blessed with my child and I feel gratitude for every moment I was given with them. On the other hand, the pain of missing my child - my greatest happiness, my life's purpose, and my best friend - is intense.

This day will forever be hard for me. I live with an emptiness that no one can fill; so I may be sad, I may be unsociable, and I may need to take a break to be by myself in a quiet place. Whatever shape my grief takes on this day, please allow me to feel the way I feel, and please follow my lead.

I find it really comforting when someone talks about my child.

I love hearing their name spoken out loud! I love hearing stories about them. Maybe you know a story I've never heard, or maybe I've heard it a hundred times before, but it really doesn't matter to me.

Thanks to the unknown author

***

Well, I made it. I survived Mother's Day. I poured myself a glass of wine, sank into the sofa, lifted my glass and made a toast:

'Here's to Tomorrow - Everyone's Day'

FATHER'S DAY

'On difficult days such as Father's Day, when we know that you won't be able to celebrate with a child who has died, please take some time to remember your baby or child. Some people use the day to celebrate the joy that being a father brought for even a short time, whereas for others it is a time to reflect and remember.'

Calum Ross, *The Lullaby Trust*

PLANNING AHEAD CAN HELP YOU COPE

On the run-up to Father's Day, as Mother's Day, shops will be filled with posters announcing the coming date. 'Happy Father's Day' will be displayed on cards - the last thing you want to see. Friends may talk about going out for a meal on 'the day'. It all reminds you of your loss.

It's important to be aware that you might be affected by these things so that hopefully you will be prepared for emotions that might resurface. Remember that it's okay to express them. Staying strong often only delays grief and acknowledging that you aren't okay is an important first step to coping with whatever you are feeling. There's no shame in admitting that you still love and miss your child.

It doesn't matter if this is your first Father's Day after losing your child, or 20 years since they died - it's okay to feel sad, angry or downright low.

Doing something as simple as writing a card to your daughter or son, or visiting a place that was special to you, can help you acknowledge that they are still a part of your life and express any emotions you are feeling in the process.

SOME THOUGHTS ABOUT FATHER'S DAY
by a bereaved Dad

On Father's Day we are told that fathers can cry, they can mourn, they don't have to be 'strong' nor hold back or 'bottle it up.' That is good advice because there are men who are inhibited and hold back. They bottle up their grief, deny themselves expression. They may appear to be weak to themselves or others, or because they feel it is their duty to be strong.

They need to know they can grieve, any way they must. They need to know that expressing their grief produces an added healing dimension to their life, with no penalty in cost, pain or time.

Many fathers grieve, but not openly; I think privacy is involved. Long ago, I decided I would mourn as I pleased, but I would do so in private. I don't care; how I mourn is no one else's business but mine. I'm sure other fathers feel the way I do and keep their mourning private.

I do grieve and I intend to keep on grieving as long as necessary. And I will go to great trouble to maintain my privacy while I grieve. If that is being inhibited, well, I just don't care.

Be careful not to be trapped by one stereotype while trying to avoid another. You need not go about wailing and gnashing your teeth in order to avoid being labeled as cold and unresponsive. If you feel comfortable crying in public, by all means do so. But if you want to be private, by all means be private. That's okay, too. This Father's Day and any day, mourn as you please.

CHRISTMAS

What can I say…
The run up to Christmas, renamed in my mind, the run away from Christmas… I remember being in a supermarket and very nearly throwing a large green cooking apple at the beaming Father Christmas when he opened his mouth to sing…

There IS light at the end of the tunnel though in this run up to Christmas - CANDLELIGHT.

OUR CANDLE LIGHTING SERVICE
by Mary Hartley
In Medway every November we have a candle lighting service for our children where we gather in a lovely venue and come together to pay tribute to them.

We read poems and sing hymns and, for the past few years, I've talked for about ten minutes about our children and our grief. There's always something, in my own life or in the media, which lights the spark of inspiration in my head.

For example, in the centenary year for the start of WW1, I saw a piece in a newspaper about the tributes to their sons and brothers that people put in their front windows and how, by 1918, more than half the houses in any street would have such a tribute. That led onto the way people must have understood and supported each other and how that was echoed in the understanding and support we give each other in TCF nowadays.

Lighting our candles together is always very special. It's a very memorable day which helps me enormously at a time when the rest of the world seems to be going 'Christmas shopping mad'.

***

And we can all light candles for our children:

CANDLE LIGHTING WORLDWIDE
I think probably we would all agree that the flame of candles is very calming. *Every year, on the Sunday two weeks before Christmas, at 7.00 pm, we members of The Compassionate Friends worldwide can light a candle for our children, so that the light travels all the way round the world. It is something we can do for them at this time, and it is comforting to know so many other bereaved parents are joining in.*

Margaret Smart

***

Christmas Cards

I bet you thought a lot about this too… Finally we wrote a short note on how we were and what we were doing, photocopied it, and put it in the Christmas cards we were still sending. Then forgot about them until the cards started coming in…

The Christmas Tree

We used to make a big occasion out of getting the Christmas tree. I remember one year it was snowing and we pulled the tree home on the sledge, all of us laughing, all of us together.

We did get a tree that first Christmas after Nikki died. I say 'we' but I took no part in that procedure and left it to the children to decorate.

Do you continue to get a tree and put decorations up in your house?

TOM'S TREE
By Julie Hope
Christmas to me was a wonderful, family occasion. I decorated

every room in the house. After the devastating loss of our son, Tom, Christmas became a non-event. The joy and love of shopping each year for new ornaments had died with Tom, I thought for ever.

Then we visited family in the USA, and our cousin, knowing how much I loved Christmas shops, took me to several. I thought rather than upset her I'd pretend to enjoy it. As I looked around I began to notice tree ornaments relating to Tom and I came out with several. That's where Tom's tree was born! From that year on I decorated a tree, small at first, with decorations all pertinent to my dearest Tom.

Now Tom's tree is much larger, as over ten years I have collected many ornaments for him and they now nestle alongside some of my older decorations. In collecting Tom's ornaments I learnt to enjoy that part of Christmas again. I can look forward to unwrapping his ornaments and decorating each year and it brings him much closer to me at that special time.

***

CHRISTMAS EVE

We lit a candle for Nikki and placed it on her grave. I put a notice up in the churchyard beforehand saying that was what we were going to do and other people were welcome to join in. The Rector came to be with us just before the midnight service. It worked, astonishingly enough, and when we came out from the service quite a lot of headstones had candles winking beside them in the dark.

Tim Claye (Nikki's Dad)

We continued to put a candle on Nikki's grave each year and it was so comforting to see the candlelight dotted around the churchyard. Then in 2003 we added another candle on the grave, for our son, Robin. It was unbelievable to see the two candles side by side throwing flickering shadows on the two inscriptions on the headstone.

DO AWAY WITH CHRISTMAS…? I wish

Our family would never be the same again. But for the sake of our other children we felt we had to make an effort. That first year we accepted an invitation from friends who lived nearby to spend the day with them; that would mean we wouldn't have to organise a turkey and all the trimmings. At home, on Christmas eve, we lit a candle for Nikki; it helped us to feel her presence amongst us.

We went for our usual Christmas and Boxing Day walks; I found this a very welcome distraction. I remember at times when I couldn't cope any more I used to run myself a warm bath, put candles round it and sink into the lovely hot water and read by candlelight. Anything to get through the day.

This poem, *Just Making the Gravy*, written at a writing workshop at one of our TCF residential weekends, reminds me vividly of how it was:

Just Making the Gravy
by Jill Yglesias
For Chloe, who died on 4th August, 2009, aged 37

The first Christmas after you died
Alice said, 'Mum, you don't have to do anything,
we'll do it all – but can you just make the gravy?'

'Of course!' I said.
One small thing. I can manage that.
I managed to make lists
*   and order food*
*   and buy presents*
*   and wrap them*

127

and dig out the stockings
and decorate the tree
and even send a few cards.

I stood by the hob.
Champagne was being passed around.
Grandchildren were happily weaving
between our legs, clutching presents and chirruping.

I had my apron on, ready.
Alice took the turkey out of the oven,
and put the roasting tin down in front of me.

'Mum, can you just make the gravy?
That's all you have to do.'
That's all I have to do.

But – I – can't

I cannot move. I cannot lift my arm.
I'm standing in front of the turkey,
paralysed
with tears pouring down my cheeks.
The first Christmas without you
I could not even manage the gravy.

Jill Yglesias

And now, over the years, we have made other rituals at Christmas to get together with family and friends to remember Chloe, still with tears, but more and more with laughter and joy too. **Jill Yglesias**

***

It helps to know what other people do for Christmas - how they cope. Here are some hints for getting through the day…

HINTS FOR THE HOLIDAY SEASON
by Darcie Sims

- *Take care of yourself physically. Eat right. Exercise (or at least watch someone else). Gift wrap some broccoli. If nothing else, jog your memory!*

- *Be realistic. It will hurt, but don't try to block bad moments. Be ready for them. Lay in a supply of tissues (a roll of toilet paper is even more efficient!). Let those hurting moments come, deal with them and let them go.*

- *Don't deny yourself the gift of healing tears. Understand that heartaches will be unpacked as you sift through the decorations, but so, too, are the warm loving memories of each piece.*

- *Think of all the 'gifts' that your loved one gave to you... joy, safety, laughter, companionship, compassion. List these 'gifts' on strips of paper, perhaps decorate the tree with them. These small strips of paper hold tangible evidence that someone lived. It is a reminder that, even though our loved one has died, we still have those gifts.*

***

This is how another 'gets through the day' and gives some very good advice...

CHRISTMAS THOUGHTS
by Maria Ahern, (James' mum)

And so it has arrived again. The winter, the festivities that come with it, the hustle and bustle that accompanies this time of year; and all I want to do is hide under a duvet. You too? Yes, I thought so.

While the rest of the world appears to be getting ready for 'the most wonderful time of the year' we are bracing ourselves for the grief triggers to hit us and developing our coping strategies. What is it for you? I've ordered more wool than is seemly and will be knee deep in crochet projects for the duration.

The most common advice we hear is 'Be kind to yourself. Do what feels right for you'. This, on the face of it, sounds like good advice, but how do you balance the conflicting needs and expectations of your family and friends with your own at such a complicated time of year? Or do you just escape? Is there any escape? Of course there is no escape, is there. All we can do is navigate it as best we can.

Do you accept that kindly meant invitation? Do you make a polite excuse and decline? Do you satisfy the needs of those around you at the cost of your own? Do you stick to old traditions or do you do it completely differently? Cards or no cards? How do you sign them? Do you include your child's name or not?

The perplexities are endless and sorry, but this next paragraph doesn't contain the answers to those questions. We all do it differently and we may change our minds from year to year. One year, you may feel more robust and find that you can cook a big meal and have a family day of sorts. Another year you may not be able to face it and retreat to your own space for a while. It is, quite literally, a movable feast.

The important thing to remember is that it doesn't matter. There are no rules. In the bigger picture, the only thing that matters, surely, is that we find a coping strategy that gets each of us through this time and out the other side. Most of us have done it before and will do it again.

But what advice would I give those for whom this is the first time? I remember my first Christmas. The pain was tangible and I found that I could barely breathe. I hadn't yet found The Compassionate Friends and looking back on it, (what I can remember for it is a bit of a blur really) I was quite literally lost. I remember thinking that I should try. That people would expect things from me. So I did. I went to a shopping centre and broke down sobbing in a department store. I might not remember much about that first Christmas, but I certainly remember the assistant trying to help me in that shop and how painful the whole experience was for me and must have been for her too.

Why did I put myself through it? To comply. That can be the only explanation for what I was doing. Placing myself in a busy shopping centre buying gifts for people when all I wanted to do was scream. Why? Who needed a gift that badly, for pity's sake? But, I wanted to be what everyone expected me to be and I was hurting myself in the process. I still can't explain why I thought I could achieve such a mammoth task. I guess it was because I didn't give myself the freedom to 'do what's right for me'. I didn't give myself permission to 'do it differently' and I certainly wasn't 'being gentle on myself' because no-one had told me I could or should.

I resolved then that things needed to be put into perspective. That I needed to find a way to balance the needs of others against my needs and to be proportionate. That's one piece of advice.

The other is the one I live by the most. **Don't be quick to take offence.** Remember, the non-bereaved speak a different language to us and a lot of what they say can get lost in translation. They also don't have the same knowledge as we do, so they don't really know what to do for the best. So, for what it's worth, my advice is to take deep breaths and shrug your shoulders. I'll give you an example. We used to get hundreds of Christmas cards before. Then, the year that James died we got six; one of those said, 'chin up' and another said, 'We hope that you are feeling better now'. As if we were recovering from a cold!

It really isn't worth getting upset about these things. People need educating, yes of course. That is why the work we do here at The Compassionate Friends is so important. We can inform people but of course what they do with that information is really a matter for them. As for us, the bereaved? Well we have enough to cope with without worrying about some Victorian traditions and how people apply them to us in our fractured world. Breathe, and shrug your shoulders.

Above all, hold on. We are all in this together and we will get through it together. The TCF Facebook groups and Forum are good places for support and the Helpline stays open even on Christmas Day, thanks to the dedication and commitment of our army of volunteers. If you need us, we are here for you.

Lastly, and most importantly, find some space for you. **Allow yourself to lean into the grief,** the missing and the longing for your child. Honour them and keep them close. We don't need to pretend. Who are we pretending for? The memories of Christmas past may sustain you in Christmas present. Let them come crashing in and allow yourself a smile remembering those happy times. We need them.

One moment, one breath, one memory at a time...

***

And to remember our children, at any kind of get together this Christmas, religious or otherwise, we can light candles and say the following:

Candle Ritual
developed by Paul Alexander TCF Otago Chapter, NZ

As we light these four candles in honour of you,
we light one for our grief, one for our courage,
one for our memories, and one for our love.

Light the first candle

This candle represents our grief. The pain of losing you is intense.
It reminds us of the depth of our love for you.

Light the second candle

This candle represents our courage - to confront our sorrow
to comfort one another - to change our lives.

Light the third candle

This light is in your memory - the times we laughed,
the times we cried - the times we were angry with each other
the silly things you did - the caring and joy you gave us.

Light the fourth candle

This light is the light of love. As we enter this holiday season,
day by day we cherish the special place in our hearts
that will always be reserved for you.

We thank you for the gift your living brought to each of us.

We love you.

NEW YEAR

Well, we didn't bargain for New Year. We made plans for that first Christmas but didn't for New Year. It took me completely by surprise. I was overcome with grief. I was going into another year and leaving my daughter behind.

I couldn't bear it. Somehow I got through New Year's Eve and then the day itself. Whenever I heard the words 'a new year' I could only think of the whole year ahead stretching out in front of me until I pulled myself together and told myself I was going to make a kind of New Year's list. Here goes, I must try to... 'Must?' There's no such word in my world these days - I'm going to have a go at the following:

1. Live one day at a time, don't try to imagine the whole year ahead

2. Look after myself, remember to eat, and go for a walk each day

3. Don't forget to breathe

4. Don't beat myself up. Laugh at myself when things don't quite go as they should

5. Put aside time to remember Robin and Nikki and know that tears are healing

6. Celebrate a good day when it comes and don't feel guilty

7. Share my story with Compassionate Friends and listen to theirs. Sharing is healing.

8. Be aware that other members of my family may grieve in different ways and at different times

9.   Pat myself on the back when I succeed - and pour myself
     a glass of wine

Well I'll have a go anyway!

I think if I had to make a New Year's wish (well, one that is possible) I could not do better than any (or all) of the ones in Sascha's poem.

New Year's Wish

*I wish you gentle days
and quiet nights.
I wish you memories
to keep you strong.
I wish you time to smile
and time for song…*

*And then,
I wish you friends
to give you love,
When you are hurt
and lost
and life is blind.
I wish you friends,
and love
and peace of mind.*
Sascha

POSITIVE THINKING

*'We cannot direct the wind
But we can adjust the sails'*

Robin used to say, 'whatever dumps on you, you can always find something to bring you joy'. I often think of him saying this. I have no control over what has happened but I can try to turn my mind to something that I can say thank you for, that will bring me joy.

Now, read through the following. Bet you've not thought of this, I hadn't and I'm trying it out myself.

THE POWER OF 'AND': HOW ONE WORD CHANGED MY LIFE
by Rachel Whalen

Five weeks after Dorothy died, my nephew was born. I remember going to our weekly therapy session and sharing this news with our therapist. Of course she wanted to know how I was feeling about his arrival. I replied that I was so happy that he was safely here but I was also happy that he lived across the country so I didn't have to see him yet.

*'And.' she replied. I looked at her puzzled. She continued, 'And. You are happy he is here AND you are happy that you don't have to see him right now. Rachel, **you don't have to choose.'***

After we left our session that day, I couldn't stop thinking about that one little word. Ever since Dorothy's death, I had found myself trying to separate my reemerging feelings of happiness from the steady depression I was in. Much like a child trying to keep their peas from touching their mashed potatoes, I wanted my feelings of devastation to be untouched by any glimmers of joy I might be feeling. I didn't think it was possible for them to co-exist.

Three simple letters changed that. I began testing out this powerful little word. Whenever I had been feeling differing emotions, I had used the word 'but' to keep them distant. What if I used 'and' to bring them together?

> *It's a beautiful day outside AND I just can't face the world today.*
> *That new picture of my nephew is so adorable AND it reminds me of how much I miss Dorothy.*
> *I'm looking forward to seeing my family AND I'm anxious to be around them.*
> *I want to talk about Dorothy AND I'm nervous about what others will have to say about her.*

'And' was slowly changing my world. That one word was giving me the freedom to experience the storm of emotions that had been quietly raging inside. I didn't have to wait for each feeling to pass over me completely, I could start feeling them in connection. Before 'and' there had been so much guilt about the happiness that was sneaking its way back into my life. Now, I had permission to let happiness start to colour the darkness of my grief.

Over the next weeks and months I exercised the power of 'and.' With the recent birth of my nephew, I found many opportunities to use my new magic word.

I'm so happy that my sister-in-law is a mother AND I wish that were me.

I want to send my nephew this cute new outfit AND I wish I could be buying clothes for my own child instead.

I want to be included in my nephew's life AND sometimes it's just too hard.

I'm so excited to be an aunt AND I'm so worried that Dorothy is going to be forgotten.

It wasn't a solution or a remedy, but it was a tool. *The burden of Dorothy's death was a heavy one. I was struggling under the weight of the emotions I had been trying to ignore and I needed help. My grief for Dorothy was never going away, but I needed something to help me carry the load throughout my life. Without a tool, I was going to be crushed. 'And' helped alleviate some of the pressure. I felt like I could breathe again. I felt like I was remembering how to live AND love.*

My husband and I recently 'graduated' from therapy. (To be clear, I will probably go back to therapy many times in my life because it is extremely important for my family and our well-being.) At our last session, my therapist asked us if we had any feedback for her. I thanked her for 'and.' She smiled and said she was glad I found it helpful in my healing.

*'I have found it helpful,' I replied. '**And** I still have a lot of healing left to do.'*

***

I have to include Steve's poem, The Scar, because for me it sums up our journey through grief.

The Scar
by Steve Carter
(Written at the Woodbrooke TCF Weekend, 12th July 2016)
My scar speaks…
> *It shouts anger.*
> *It screams pain.*
> *It says to the healer, 'Why me? Why this wound so deep?*
> *Do not touch me, because I fear the searing pain.'*
And the healer said to me…

'I will heal your wound and yet you will not know that
I have done so.
Now look again.'
And now my scar speaks new words. It speaks softly to others.
It says to them...
'Look! Where there was weakness, I am now strength.
Where there was ugliness, I have become beauty.
Where there were tears, I scatter radiance.'
My scar will always be with me - a sign forever that, where
there was death, there is new, healing life.

***

Positive thinking often starts with becoming aware of self talk - the thoughts that run through your head. I try to become aware of my thoughts and if they are negative and making me feel low, I try to change the direction of my thoughts, perhaps by remembering one particular thing about Nikki and Robin that makes me smile. I try to see humour in everyday happenings and give myself permission to smile or laugh, especially during difficult times. It certainly helps - give it a go.

> *'Treat yourself like you would a five-year-old child*
> *you adore. Children need love, affection, nurturing*
> *and our attention. Try giving that to yourselves*
> *wholeheartedly.'*

Do you feel sorry for yourself at times? I must admit I can catch myself feeling like this. And then what happens? My thoughts go into a downward spiral and my mood darkens, it gets a hold on me and I find myself conjuring up the next thing that can go wrong...

PICKING MYSELF UP
by Pat Allen

Being in the caring professions, I have read a great deal about bereavement. We are told our grief falls into rough stages, or components as one expert calls them:

Shock, disbelief, searching, anger, depression, apathy and finally some acceptance. Yes, I suppose I knew all those things myself recently. Looking back it all seems a muddled nightmare. I couldn't even begin to plot the stages.

Nearly two years later life is good again, the sun shines and I look forward. I am left, however, with a component that the experts never mentioned. Self Pity. An old enemy, it stalks me night and day. I know it to be completely evil and destructive. The only way to deal with it is to be totally ruthless.

I try never to let it get a hold. It is unproductive, I am sure it breeds self doubt and makes us less effective and resourceful. Self pity encourages us to look for the next disaster, the next tragedy. Is that a way to live?

Feeling sorry for myself is most likely to happen when I am alone. If it does I attack head on. I can be observed shouting down the wind, 'Get the hell out of it!' Sometimes that works. If it doesn't I accept that I lost that round.

I pick myself up, dust myself down, and start all over again.

***

So we have to make a choice. Are we going to spend the rest of our lives sinking down on the sofa, feeling hopeless and in so doing, affect those around us? Or are we going to get up and try to make the most of the life we have.

My Son, My Son

I don't know why
I'll never know why.
I don't have to know why.
I don't have to like it.

What I do have to do is make a
Choice about my living.
The choice is mine.
I can go on living

Valuing every moment
In a way I never did before
Or I can be destroyed by it
And, in turn, destroy others.

I thought I was immortal,
That my family and my children were also.
That tragedy happened only to others.
But I know now that life is tenuous
And valuable.

So I am choosing to go on living.
Making the most of time I have
Valuing my family and friends
In a way never possible before.
Iris Bolton, *TCF Western Australia*

So let's give life a go. Let's do our best to put one foot in front of the other in the realisation that our life is what we make it.

Now, thinking positively, imagine yourself as a rather blunt pencil:

WHAT THE PENCIL MAKER TOLD THE PENCIL

1. *Everything you do will always leave a mark.*
2. *You can always correct the mistakes you make.*
3. *What is important is what is inside you.*
4. *In life, you will undergo painful sharpening, which will only make you better.*
5. *To be the best pencil, you must allow yourself to be held and guided by the hand that holds you.*

We all need to be constantly sharpened. This parable may encourage you to know that you are a special person, with unique talents and abilities. Only you can fulfil the purpose which you were born to accomplish.

Never allow yourself to get discouraged and think that your life is insignificant and cannot be changed. Like the pencil, always remember that the most important part of who you are, is what's inside you.

And finally, a Native American story:

TWO WOLVES
A grandfather was talking to his grandson. 'A fight is going on inside me,' he said to the boy.

'It is a terrible fight and it is between two wolves.

'One wolf is evil and ugly: he is anger, envy, war, greed, self-pity, sorrow, regret, guilt, resentment, inferiority, lies, false pride, superiority, selfishness and arrogance.

'The other wolf is beautiful and good: he is friendly, joyful, peace, love, hope, serenity, humility, kindness, benevolence, justice, fairness, empathy, generosity, truth, compassion, gratitude, and deep vision.

'This same fight is going on inside you, and inside every other human as well.'

The grandson thought deeply of what his grandfather had

said. Then he finally asked, 'So Grandfather, which wolf will win?'

The grandfather quietly replied, 'The one that you feed.'

***

I found this story simple and very wise. Which wolf was I feeding? Was I still feeding the part of me that remained consumed by my grief with consequent feelings of hopelessness and inability to tackle life? Or was I feeding the part of me that could look life in the eye and say, 'Right, you've thrown the worst thing possible at me. Now, one step at a time, I'm going to find a way to live a positive life, acknowledging what has happened, but determined to live my life with hope, love and meaning.'

EATING

I have just had an ENORMOUS slice of the sponge cake I make frequently. It has a generous filling of raspberry jam in the middle and I'm feeling better already. I tell myself that as well as sugar and delicious jam it also has eggs and flour which are very nourishing. When I feel in need of extra nourishing, I add strawberries or raspberries and double cream; the result is mouth watering… and, I can hear you say, fattening.

But especially when we are initially bereaved we do need to remind ourselves to eat. Easier said than done. Who cares about food when our child has just died. And although it seems the hardest thing in the world, we've got to get up in the morning and put one foot in front of the other and we need fuel to do this. I shall always be grateful to friends who came round after Nikki, and then Robin, died, with a hearty casserole or a very welcome cake. They were desperately needed, as our fridge was bare.

Now I know those of you who are newly bereaved may not be able to take in the following recipe for the moment, but for some of you further along the road of grief, in case you're looking for something to get stuck in to - perhaps a cake to take round to newly bereaved parents - why don't you have a go at this:

My Sponge Cake Recipe
6 oz self raising flour,
6 oz Stork margarine
5 oz golden caster sugar
a very large teaspoon of baking powder
3 eggs, weighing between 6.0 oz and 6.4 oz with shells on
Two 7in round baking tins

I sift the flour and stick it, together with the baking powder, sugar, margarine and eggs, into a mixer and let it whizz
Meanwhile I turn my fan oven on to 160 degrees (180 if it's not a fan)
I let the mixer whizz for as long as it takes my oven to heat up - that's important
I dollop the mixture into the baking tins
Put the tins in the centre of the oven
Bake for 30 mins
Take out and allow to stand for a couple of minutes then
Turn out onto a rack to cool
I spread with raspberry jam. You choose whichever jam you like then sandwich together and
EAT

Some notes which I think are important
I only use 5 oz of sugar instead of 6 oz. I've had several comments: 'I like your sponge, cos it's not too sweet'.
After weighing the flour, the scales read 6.0 oz. I add the baking powder until the scales read 6.3 oz. I don't know if this is a large teaspoon, or two.
I always use margarine, always Stork, and never butter. This makes the cake lighter.
Make sure you let the mixture whizz for a good time.
I use paper liners and I grease the bottom of the liners so that the cake comes out easily.

That's it, I think. If you have a go, good luck - and tuck in.

Something less complicated but nourishing, if it's been one of those days and you can't face cooking or even rummaging in the freezer for one of those precooked forgotten items lurking there, is a banana and a glass of milk. So if friends want to know if they can get you anything from the shop, give them a list, but make sure bananas and a carton of milk are on it - as well as that bottle of wine.

I still find myself going to the supermarket and seeing things that Robin or Nikki used to like, and sometimes picking them up and putting them in my trolley. Do you find yourself doing that too?

SENTIMENTAL, SILLY, MAD? I DON'T THINK SO
by Eileen Whatmough

Sometimes I fear for my sanity. It is now more than nine years since I lost my beloved son, Oliver, and I am still shopping with his tastes in mind! Yesterday I bought a malt loaf; Oliver loved malt loaf. Now, I am supposed to be on a diet, but during the course of the day that malt loaf disappeared - just a couple of slices with each cup of coffee - and oh, how I enjoyed it, savouring memories of happy times with every mouthful.

I buy Olivio margarine simply because of the name - not quite Oliver but almost - and I buy Country Life butter because Oliver could mimic the West Country accent so well and make me laugh. I smile every time I reach for the packet.

*Those are just three items - there are several others - so you see why I wonder about my state of mind. But deep down I know that all these small idiosyncrasies are merely strategies helping me, in fact, to keep my sanity. I think that none of us should worry about how we **ought** to be feeling - **and whatever** brings comfort, happy memories and just a moment or two of relief from the loneliness of loss - just do it, and enjoy it.*

EXERCISE

*'Exercise can help even the newly bereaved. Just sitting quietly
and breathing slowly and deeply, in and out, for a certain time each day.
Stretching is also helpful and not too taxing in the early days.'*

Ok, let's start with Walking. It's good for us, we've all been told that. But some days all I want to do is sit in my comfy armchair, just thinking about it. If I could manage to haul myself up, go out into the fresh air and put one foot in front of the other - and keep doing it, then I'm walking.

I try and do a half hour walk each day (I'm afraid I frequently don't manage it!). I often use two hiking sticks and find them extremely helpful as I have COPD which means my lungs are not as efficient as they should be, especially when the path goes upwards, which it frequently does living amongst the Chiltern hills.

Mind you, that's nothing compared to Wales. Last year I did a couple of weeks' Welsh course in Aberystwyth which, apart from the lovely promenade and coast, is built on a hill and everywhere is all up and down. Thank goodness I have a car!

I've discovered some interesting facts about walking:
- The foot's impact during walking sends pressure waves through the arteries that significantly modify and can increase the supply of blood to the brain.
- This in turn triggers things such as endorphins and serotonin which help to lift our mood.
- It can give us a sense of purpose and a sense of control.

DID YOU KNOW?
by Bryan Clover

My counsellor told me that walking is particularly good for bereaved parents because it uses both sides of the brain, which in turn helps you to process the grief more effectively. She said that if you find gardening therapeutic, or any other activity then make sure that you use both hands - for example, when pruning roses, don't just use the clippers in your right hand, but hold the stalk with your left so that you make a coordinated action, and therefore use both sides of the brain once again.

✳✳✳

Terry Ahern whose son, James, died in a road traffic accident, walks and walks. He now also leads walks around London in the spring and summer which are proving very popular.

WALKING
by Terry Ahern

Since losing James, walking has been a godsend to me. Walking in a group or alone, or a combination of both, brings comfort and enjoyment. We are often told that walking is good for our physical and mental wellbeing; this is even more important when trying to cope with the loss of a child. We need to look after ourselves.

In the early days when I was finding it difficult to sleep, I found that being tired after a walk made it easier to rest. Being close to nature brings me closer to James. I find the term 'Walking Meditation' very true. If I'm looking at buildings or places of interest, this occupies my thoughts and I love to learn new facts.

Walking can be a social experience too. Talking about the walk, the weather and what you see, is an easy conversation and avoids difficult topics. Of course, walking with other bereaved parents gives another layer of comfort, it means everyone can relax, talk freely about their children and their feelings.

***

I used to walk a lot when I was younger, usually on the beautiful Gower coast in South Wales where I was brought up. It would often be a morning or afternoon walk, sometimes a whole day - but I have never tried to walk for five weeks on end!

A JOURNEY TO THE HEART
by Caroline Vodden
In memory of Ben, 6ᵗʰ January 1995 - 12ᵗʰ December 2006

I first heard about the Camino de Santiago in 2009, and last year, gifted with a three month sabbatical from work, I had a 'now or never' opportunity to walk it myself. On 13th May I took the train to the Eurostar Terminal at St Pancras where a large neon sign beneath the station clock illuminated the words: 'I want my time with you'. With whom? Perhaps with myself... Our son Ben took his own life just before his 12th birthday. The pain of loss has lessened on a day-to-day basis as we have adjusted to our 'new normality' but it still resurfaces acutely from time to time and the love we feel for Ben is undiminished.

After a night in Saint-Jean-Pied-de-Port in the French Pyrenees, I took the first tentative steps on my 800km pilgrimage to Santiago. I soon found a real freedom in the simple daily pattern of walking, eating, sleeping, and sometimes talking with fellow pilgrims.

Even on the first day I found I was enjoying the solitude, listening to the birdsong and feasting my eyes on the beauty of the spring flowers. By Day 4 I found to my surprise that I was actually enjoying my own company as I traversed a mountainous ridge and descended a rocky path carpeted with wild thyme. These were the halcyon days. By the end of the first week I had developed a sore Achilles tendon, requiring me to lighten the contents of my rucksack and offload all but the absolute essentials, finding a strange lightening of the heart in the process.

On Day 11, I found myself in a hostel with just one other pilgrim, an older Frenchman whose wife had died a few months before. We struck up a conversation and before long I was telling him about Ben and about how I felt unable to love myself. Tears flowed and with great tenderness and compassion he urged me, 'Ouvre ta coeur', open your heart. The trouble was I did not know how.

Over the next few days I reflected on this conversation and looked back over my life in search of answers. On Day 21 I left the hostel before dawn and, as the warming sun caused the mist to rise, my tears started to fall. For two hours I wept and sobbed as the realisation dawned that my Camino journey was a search for my lost self. When Ben died, my heart died and love was buried. Life became a daily determination just to survive. Compassion was born, and empathy, but my heart turned to stone, petrified and frozen.

Further conversations followed with other pilgrims as we shared our personal stories and struggles and helped each other along the way. There was a new spring in my step and the world seemed brighter, the birds singing more sweetly, the flowers more colourful, and as I walked through the wheat fields I found myself singing John Crum's Easter hymn: 'Fields of our hearts that dead and bare have been: Love is come again, like wheat that springs up green.' After existing in a zombie state my heart was softening and I began to feel alive for the first time in many years.

Arriving at the Cruz de Hierro, the iron cross high on the Montes de Leon, I was ready to lay down the stone I had brought with me from home, one that Ben had collected, representing the burden I had carried for twelve years. A stone with a hole in the middle, like the Ben-shaped hole in my heart which was now ready to be filled again with love.

I had found a sense of peace and could look forward.

The next ten days were spent getting to know myself again and enjoying the walk through vineyards and stunning mountain scenery. I realised it was the first time I had really been able to take time to process the grief of losing Ben. I cried tears of regret and deep sadness and love, but also of release and joy.

Reaching Santiago de Compostela at the end of five weeks' walking, I said goodbye to the strangers who had become friends, then continued to the coast at Finisterre to dip in the ocean and watch the sun sink over the western horizon. Then I returned to Santiago, where a kindly nun gave me a poem which summed up the inner journey made possible by my outward pilgrimage: 'Beloved is where you begin.' Now I was able to love myself and to know God who is Love, because I felt free to love again.

***

I can only have great admiration for anyone who undertakes such an arduous physical and deeply spiritual journey. Some of us, however, have a meaningful destination on our doorstep.

THE HEARTSTONE: *Making a mini-pilgrimage*
by Ian Campbell

The walk my wife, Margaret, and I do several times a week has become meaningful enough to us to be called a pilgrimage. We live just behind the Promenade at the western edge of

Portobello, 'Edinburgh's Seaside', so there were few days we didn't go on to the beach. It became a place of healing.

We walk, south-east, to the Joppa end and from there it's about a quarter of a mile inland to Portobello Cemetery where Hugh is buried. Being able to walk to his grave has been a comfort. At high tide, we walk on the Prom instead and would look down, about three quarters of the way along, at a little cove with a patch of shingle and a few boulders.

It looked interesting and eventually we made our way to this little beach at low tide to poke about the flotsam and jetsam. One of the boulders, slightly detached from the rest, was perfect for sitting on and it became our habit to pause there on the walks to have a few moments contemplating the sea and remembering Hugh.

After a few visits, we noticed that this stone was heart-shaped and so christened it the 'Heartstone'. Then we spotted a vertical line running across the stone and so thought of it as a broken heart. Finally we discerned a faint horizontal line, making a cross, and so it became, inevitably for us as Catholics, the Sacred Heart of Jesus.

On some occasions we visited, there would be stones and shells left on it by the receding tides or dropped by seabirds. They looked like offerings and we began at first to place either a stone or a shell in memory of Hugh, and then gradually added more - for ourselves and our older son, Thomas. Sometimes we would place others for people in our thoughts and prayers.

I am very grateful to have experienced the gradual unfolding of this as a meaningful destination on our doorstep, investing what could have been a pleasant but routine walk with the significance of a pilgrimage. The only drawback has been that I came to feel it would be irreverent to sit on the Sacred Heart and none of the other boulders has proved so accommodating.

***

RUNNING
When you're running you're processing hurt and pain. You raise your heart rate and sweat out the toxins. It's how the body cries.

Carolyn Brice, our wonderful CEO of The Compassionate Friends, found running brought purpose to her life and seemed to give her a reason to go on when her beloved daughter, Rosie, died.

RUNNING TO HOPE
by Carolyn Brice

My daughter, Rosie, was my first baby and was born in May when the beautiful blossom makes it appearance. When she died aged nine and a half suddenly from a brain aneurysm I didn't have any idea how I would be able to survive.

Another bereaved parent did say to me in those early days that eventually I would be able to live, laugh and love again, able to remember Rosie with a smile for the happy memories, rather than always through the pain and grief of her loss. I didn't believe them - in fact I was angry that they could think that I could do any of those things without my child - I felt they must have not loved their child as much as I loved and adored Rosie. I have found, however, that they were right - and I do now have a fulfilling, hopeful 'happy' life again after 13 years without my daughter physically with me.

When Rosie first died I could not bear to be outdoors - particularly in spring or summer - sunny days, when all the flowers are blooming, the leaves are lush and verdant, and new life is everywhere around. I would shut myself away on these days, preferring the dark and dank days full of rain and cloud, which more accurately suited my mood.

The spring and summer seasons and the natural world seemed to be 'mocking me' - shoving in my face this new, blossoming plant and animal life, throwing into stark contrast the fact that my spring baby was not here. Rosie loved the natural world… as a toddler she adored flowers (many times I had to stop her picking the daffodils in our local park!) and as she grew she memorised all the names of the plants and flowers (her granny had taught her). She loved mucking around in the garden, planting and digging, and I can still see her and her sister standing under blossom trees when the wind blew, loving the feeling of blossom 'snow' falling and swirling around them.

A few years after Rosie died, my surviving daughter, Natalie, was anxious about a cross-country run in which she was going to have to participate in her new secondary school. She asked me if I would practice running with her. What I haven't told you is that since my teenage years I had been an exercise-phobe. In fact, I was very happy when I left school as I knew I wouldn't ever have to take part in any exercise ever again! So, I immediately said to Natalie that there was absolutely no way I was going to run with her, and in any case I didn't enjoy spending time outdoors because of the associations with Rosie, and I would have to do both.

However, she pleaded with me, as no one else would run with her, and in the end I told her that I would do it, but I would go at my own pace, and stop when I wanted, and that she was not to wait for me. Off we went, I wore my old trainers (I had them since my teenage years - never worn since leaving school!) - and she was ahead most of the time! Although it was hard work for someone as unfit as me, I strangely found it hugely mood enhancing and even a little bit enjoyable. Especially the feeling afterwards and the real 'lift' it gave me.

So, I carried on. I carried on even after Natalie had completed her school cross country runs and no longer wanted to practice or run again... It seemed to give me a reason to go on (Some sort of purpose to my life was something that I had struggled with in the early years after Rosie's death). I had time to think while running and even if that thinking was about my girl, it also strangely cleared my head and relieved stress and anxiety.

Gradually as I increased my pace and length of time running I started to look up - notice the flowers, the greenery, the sky. Although I still felt the pain of sadness in the natural world I could now 'see' Rosie - and happy and joyful memories of her smelling the flowers, dancing on the grass, playing in the garden came slowly back. Instead of mocking and taunting me, the bursting into life of the natural world that the spring and summer brings is now a source of hope and light, and I feel 'close' to Rosie. We got a dog - a working cocker spaniel - who loved to run - and she would trot alongside me enjoying the sun, the park and river path.

And so it has been that through her little sister, running has brought Rosie close to me, helped her to live 'inside' me and given me hope. Thank goodness.

***

SWIMMING
At the moment I can't manage to do a length without stopping and hanging on to the side to get my breath back. So I often go into the Dolphin pool - the little ones' pool - and splash about there. For me, it's about exercise rather than swimming. But I do feel better after the session. It helps my breathing and it makes me feel alive and ready to take on the next task.

MY ANTI-DEPRESSANT
by Jane Edmonds

I go swimming. For me that's my anti-depressant. A plunge into cold water that proves that I'm still alive... my own wake up call to the hard reality that there's nothing to be done about Josh's death except to carry on living. Then there's the rhythm of the stroke, the breath, the sound of the water, all taking me to another world where for a moment, life and all its responsibilities is reduced to the mechanics of pure existence - life which is as close to death and to Josh as I dare go. I swim therefore I am.

***

CYCLING

I do have a bicycle but I'm afraid it's leaning against the wall in my garage and doesn't get to go out for a ride these days. So I looked around for someone who cycles and at a TCF pastoral committee meeting I nabbed Robert. Here's how he started to cycle...

CYCLING TO REMEMBER
by Robert Treadgold

Just before my son, Matthew, died suddenly at the age of 32, he helped me choose a cycle to start me on the road to better fitness. He had been a fairly keen cyclist for a long time but in truth, I was at the 'reluctant' end of the scale. I found it rather boring, hard going and, usually, inconvenient.

'Just do little and often Dad', was his advice. OK I thought, I will. So, for a while I did. Then came the phone call every parent dreads and many of us in TCF have received.

Strangely, it wasn't too long after he died, perhaps a few weeks, that I was almost compelled to get back on my bike. At that time I cycled alone, but I found the relative peace of the lanes near where I live and a strong sense of a connection back to those conversations with him, reassuring and somehow comforting. I felt now that I was doing this for a number of reasons, not just for fitness improvement.

Someone told me early on, that sleep, food and exercise are crucial to taking those early steps on the 'Path not Chosen'. Easily said and maybe obvious but how very true. I was now doing this mostly because I simply had to, for Matthew. To show him that I could do it and to make him proud.

During one of my last conversations with him, he asked me if I was going to set myself a goal. Half jokingly I said, 'I wonder if I could ever cycle the length of a marathon quicker than the world record holder takes to run it?!'. Now, to any experienced or even some inexperienced cyclists, that's a Sunday afternoon warm up. But to me, at that time, me who got bored after half an hour and sore very soon after, it was merely words and never likely to be a reality.

Months later, when I was still doing 'little and often', I joined a cycling club. I was really beginning to enjoy this. Matt was, and always will be, with me every mile I cycle.

One cycle ride, with about eight other club members, felt rather longer and a bit quicker than usual. Was it my lack of fitness or that fish and chips I'd had the day before, I wondered. I thought little more of it until we returned to the car park at the end of the evening. I didn't have 'an app' or on board speed/ distance recorder at the time so asked the leader how far and time taken. 'Just over 26 miles in 1 hour 54 minutes', she said. Until then it didn't even occur to me that I might be about to achieve my goal thought up and inspired by Matthew. But, achieve it I had. I cried on the way home, bitter sweet tears, but I knew then that I was proud and that Matthew was also.

My next goal ? To do it on his bike that I have kept in storage waiting for me to have the courage to get on board, to sit where he sat, and to achieve something that we talked about, together.

***

So ok, I don't cycle now, but I walk. Sometimes I go up to the woods nearby; there's a circular path through a wooded area and if I do the circuit twice that's my half hour done. It's so lovely there; it's shady in the hot weather and it shelters me when it's raining. It leaves me with a feeling of energy.

But it's a long time since I've played tennis.

PLAYING TENNIS
by Liz Farmilo

I play tennis and I can take out all my frustrations on that small yellow ball. It also gives me the chance to concentrate on something else, which gives me a momentary break from the grief, plus the social side of seeing friends and also getting some fresh air. There is something about using my body as well as my mind which helps too.

MICHAEL WALFORD-GRANT lost his only son, William, aged 13, some years ago. Michael is a volunteer on the TCF Helpline and plays squash - something I've never tried. He says:

I play Squash. Squash is one of the very rare sports that requires the following to play it to a high standard:
- *Fitness*
- *Skill*
- *Tactics*
- *Psychology*
- *1 to 1 dual / competitiveness / 'nowhere to hide'*

Playing can be both exhilarating and hugely frustrating.

It provides a focus and you have to concentrate: if you lose this concentration when playing, you can lose to an inferior opponent. This is what made the game a good distraction and focus for me during the bereavement process.

Running a Squash team and being Chairman of the committee results in work and tasks that need to be done, so this consumes time, which as you know is often a good distraction from the reality of what you are living through. Also, both of the above force you to go out, socialise, and communicate with people, even on those nights when you really don't fancy it.

I also run and cycle. I took part in the 102 mile ride in North Norfolk!

***

I exercise my fingers - every day. I play scales and arpeggios on the piano, not for very long, just so I can feel I'm keeping my fingers in working order. And then some days I just sit and play… including what I call my 'doodle'. I used to play the guitar so am used to thinking in chords, so I made my doodle up out of the chords, F, G minor, B flat and C7.

I played it on a baby grand in the foyer of Raffles Hospital in Singapore where Robin was being treated. When I play it now it's as though I'm sharing it with him. At one Candle Lighting Ceremony on a TCF weekend, we couldn't get the CD player to work, so while everyone lit their candles in memory of their children, I played my doodle. …It brought Robin very much into the room with us.

If all these energetic exercises are too much for you at the moment, try a gentle walk in the garden. Do some arm and leg stretches while you're sitting in your chair. When you're watching TV get up during the adverts to get yourself a glass of water or make a cup of tea. Stick your tongue out against the world. Give a big yawn, yawning is good for you.

'Whether you're exercising all of you or bits of you, there is no right or wrong way to exercise, what works best for you is ok.'

GARDENING

'The mystery of both grief and my garden is: the thing that is happening when it looks like nothing is happening.'

I hated spring for many years; both Nikki and Robin died in March. Everything was springing back into life, but I had to bury my children. Both times I didn't know how I was going to survive. I felt unbelievable pain and hopelessness…

But Robin used to sit in the garden, at the little white table with his cup of tea, reading the newspaper and for me, at that time, it seemed the natural place to be. Gradually I started to plant the odd pansy here and there to try to bring some colour into my life.

Sundays were very hard, I didn't know what to do on my own with a day that used to be a family together day. I took to visiting garden centres, wandering around in a daze, stopping to have a cup of coffee, wandering around again. One time, I found a rose, a pink one, called Compassion. I had to buy it. I brought it home, made the effort and planted it. Thirty-two years later it still blooms every year from June to November.

And I discovered Crocs. You don't have to reach down to pull them on, you don't have to tie laces; you just step out of your shoes - or slippers - and step into Crocs. They're like the business end of wellingtons without the long bit you have to pull up.

Now, many years later I enjoy the doing of it all. Believe it or not, I enjoy weeding. I don't have to think too hard. I don't have to think how far to cut it back or where I should plant it. If it's a weed I pull it up.

Our gardens, just by being there when we wake up each morning, can help us face the coming day…

> 'Everything that slows us down and forces
> patience,
> everything that sets us back into the slow circles of
> nature, is a help.
> Gardening is an instrument of grace.'
> May Strain

It's also a very good place to sit and enjoy a cup of tea while planning what to grow next.

GARDENING
by Marion Cameron

I have always loved gardening, but had no energy to even plant my potatoes that first year. I found just sitting in the garden with a cuppa, and planning what to grow next helped me.

Snowdrops, daffodils, tulips, anemones and lilies are my favourite bulbs…BUT Sweet Peas are my absolute favourites!

My other activity in the garden is collecting leaves in the Autumn and bagging them up to store over the winter… so in a few weeks time I will be spreading that lovely stuff over my borders to keep the weeds down and enrich the soil…

***

And I know I"m not the only one who picks flowers from the garden to put on the grave:

FLOWERS FOR LEE
by Eileen Foreman

Lee spent a lot of his young life in the garden, so, many of the flowers I take to his grave are from my garden. I choose what I call 'young flowers', tete-a-tete miniature double daffodils, and snowdrops, because he was young. In the spring I take blue primroses and in the autumn, blue echinops (globe thistle) because he had the most lovely blue eyes. Picking the flowers from my garden and taking them to Lee's grave helps me greatly.

***

When our life has been shattered and we're trying to pick up the pieces, sometimes gardening can give us a new outlook on life.

A BIT OF A MIRACLE
by Kelly Cooper

Before I lost my son Cameron, my only child, to a cancerous brain tumour at the age of 13, I only needed to look at a plant and it would die. What happened after was a bit of a miracle. Online I ordered some Rose seeds that you could name and register, so they were registered as 'Cameron Rose' .

I did not expect much from past performance, but to my surprise they grew into beautiful roses. I was delighted that I had managed to nurture these tiny seeds and it gave me great pleasure to see them bloom repeatedly. So I embarked on a project to renew my garden. Being outside alone with my own thoughts and gardening seemed to give me an inner peace I had not felt before. If a plant died or didn't work properly I shrugged it off and tried something else.

Now my garden is my pride and joy and I cannot wait for the spring and summer months to arrive for me to get out there. I look forward to visiting our local garden show, with the colours that I now appreciate so much. Just to sit in the garden with a cup of tea, the sun on my face, with time to breathe and think of Cameron is just wonderful.

***

And sometimes just being close to nature can bring us a sense of constancy and infinite peace.

SITTING IN THE GARDEN
by Sylvia Hornby

I have loved flowers but since Chris's tragic death by drowning in the summer of 1988, I have come to see them in a completely different light. Only this morning I sat in the garden on a beautiful sunny day in March, just staring in wonder at some lovely crocuses and snowdrops and this gave me immense peace.

A NEVER-ENDING CYCLE
by Kirsti A Dyer

Being in nature one becomes aware of the infinite circle of life. There is evidence of decay, destruction and death; there are also examples of rejuvenation, restoration, and renewal. The never-ending cycle of birth, life, death and rebirth can put life and death into perspective and, after experiencing a life changing loss or a death, can impart a sense of constancy.

KNITTING AND CROCHETING

I have taken up knitting again. I hadn't done any for many years; there were so many other things with which to occupy myself. But being offered needles and wool at a knitting group on one of our residential weekends for newly bereaved parents in Derbyshire, I decided to join in.

I cast on a small number of stitches and started. I didn't know if I was making anything in particular or just knitting row after row. It didn't matter. What was important to me was that my fingers were working away. I didn't have to think. They just kept going.

Doing anything together in an atmosphere of understanding is healing, but this was the first time I'd tried knitting together with others. Repetitive, safe, able to chat at the same time, nattering sometimes about our children, sometimes about what we'd had for lunch. Everything accepted, everyone accepted, running smoothly - most of the time…

Together

Our knitting circle
At Willersley,
Needles clicking
Tongues chattering
Knitting together in words
As well as in wool.

Until
I dropped a stitch,
Couldn't pick it up
Couldn't cope.
With your smile, kindly,

Gently, you lifted
Needles from my grasp,
Picked us up.

Again, needles clicking,
Tongues chattering,
Naming ourselves
'Knitting nutters',
Heaving with laughter
Together, all of us
In stitches.

Gina Claye

Maria Ahern, our current chair of TCF, believes knitting or crocheting or other craft activities - something that goes on and on - is calming and therapeutic. She has tried to get her husband, Terry, to try knitting but he won't have it; he goes walking, mile after mile. He says it's the same thing, repetitive and therapeutic. I can't help feeling that walking is like knitting with legs.

CURL UP AND CROCHET
by Maria Ahern, (James' Mum)
I instinctively turned to knitting and crochet after losing James. I've always been a person who has to do things and can't sit still, yet I found that the weight of grief was preventing me from doing anything. My energy levels were depleted and all I wanted to do was to curl up on the sofa and let life pass me by.

I can't quite remember why I reached from that sofa to a long forgotten project I had started before, but I did. The repetition of the stitching gave me a sense of purpose and I began to knit as a way of self comfort and to pass the time. The research into the benefits of this and other crafts are well documented but for the grieving, it is even more beneficial.

It reminds me of a poem that Gina has written, 'Carpe Diem - Seize the Day'. It speaks of giving yourself permission to do nothing and not feel guilty for your understandable lethargy. Nevertheless, I struggled with 'doing nothing', but I struggled even more to do anything, and the weight of all this caused more conflict in my mind. So I found crochet a perfect antidote.

Although I was a proficient knitter, I only had a very basic and fundamental knowledge of crochet so I decided that I could tax myself a little and develop my skills. I needed to do something but I just didn't have the enthusiasm to move from my adopted position 'in my cave, on my sofa'. Learning to crochet grabbed my attention so I asked my mum to start me up. I had grown up watching her make intricate lace objects and beautiful crochet items and the added benefit of this is that it engaged her too.

I have now developed my knowledge and I have made some lovely items. Not the lace that my mum makes, I stick to making, dare I say it, more modern items. But there is so much creative fun to be had, and with crochet, projects seem to finish in half the time.

I found that crochet is much easier than knitting as it lends itself more to sporadic bursts of crafting. For example, **you can't drop a stitch in crochet, since there is only one on the hook at any time.** *You can be creative when the mood takes you and you can just hold it in your lap when staring into space or when having a nap seems like a more preferable pastime. You can do a little bit and put it down without fear that some of it will be unravelled as you can always just pick up the last stitch. It is very like the bursts and waves of grief and can be used as an anchor when you feel that you can't face anything more complex but you want an excuse to escape.*

The end benefit is that you can make some lovely little gifts and

I have found it very easy and quick to construct some for all those supportive friends who have held me up and stopped me unravelling!!

When I have had a particularly difficult day or the feelings of grief are particularly overwhelming, the crochet becomes a tool for mindfulness. Now I use it to calm my mind and try and recover my equilibrium.

Given the rapid depletion of my concentration levels in those early months, I was pleased to have a hobby that I could pick up and put down at will. I often now just sit curled up, holding my crochet in my lap staring into space, yet just by holding that little hook and yarn I somehow feel purposeful. And also I feel less guilty about spending too long in my curled up position.

I often convince myself that having spent an hour or two making a little gift basket or baby blanket is an hour or two well spent. These are my favourite projects at the moment. Baby blankets and baskets for baby showers. James' cousins and friends are having children of their own now and I've had labels made which say "JamieKiss" on them so that each craft gift that I make is given with a special young man firmly in mind and as a token of love.

See? So what if I put off other more tedious chores when I can sit in my own space with my memories and make something that will make someone smile. The chores can wait!

***

Maria has tried to teach me to crochet but so far she hasn't managed it. I must have another go!

I have a deep admiration for people who can knit something complicated, like my mother used to do. In fact she stopped using patterns; she had so much experience she would make it up as she went along, frequently using up all the odd bits of wool. That's why I've got a sweater of many different colours and different patterns.

At one National Gathering I sat in the lounge with Mary Hartley, our wonderful TCF Librarian. Not only could she do complicated knitting with ease, she could talk at the same time! I continued to knit my simple scarf in ordinary garter stitch while her fingers flew.

KNITTING
by Mary Hartley

My grandmother taught me to knit when I was about four years old and it's something I find very relaxing. After my daughter died I couldn't be bothered for quite a while but then her sister, quite cleverly with hindsight, turned up with a pattern and a load of wool and pleaded with me to make her a jumper. I have to say I was a bit cross at first, and dumped it all in a corner, but I kept looking at it and eventually picked it up and started to knit and I'm very glad I did.

Because it's something I've been doing for nearly all of my life, I don't have to think about knitting or even look at my hands because they just work away by themselves on a very well oiled groove. **For months I'd been in a state of continual mental and physical tension and suddenly I felt myself relaxing and calming down for an hour or two.**

I found I could watch TV again or listen to audio tapes or music. I didn't retain much from what I'd watched or listened to but that didn't matter. I think, although knitting was therapeutic for me, it could apply to any sort of craft which engages you in an almost mindless sort of way. It might be crochet, cross stitch, painting or even something like a jigsaw puzzle. Anything that can ease the stress and the tension, even if it's only for a little while, must be beneficial.

KNITTING WITH ARTHRITIS
The internet is amazing. I came across a page in 'Love Knitting', entitled Knitting with arthritis. So you can skip the following until you feel you need it!

- Hold your hands in warm water for a while before picking up the needles.

- Knit in short bursts and don't overdo it; it will build up your overall stamina.

- Try using alternative needles to metal. Bamboo and birch would be much better as they are lighter and warmer to the touch.

- Stick to using wool and wool blends because they're easier to manoeuvre due to their elasticated properties.

- Knit flat on a circular needle so that the weight of your knitting doesn't put strain on your wrists.

KNITTING FOR CHARITY
I'm thinking of having a go at this. I've been told that knitting for those more in need than yourself can dramatically change your perspective on life, It can subtly change your thinking - you become aware that you have the ability and power to improve the lives of those worse off than yourself, and in so doing, your own.

CRAFT

Apart from knitting, the only other craft I do is embroidery. My mother was very skilful and created wonderful embroidered clothes, table cloths and cushions. I have some of her beautiful cushions in my sitting room. She passed on her knowledge to me and I have various items I've embroidered including a skirt I wear in the summer, but my skill is no match for hers.

I'm always amazed by the creations people are able to conjure up out of pieces of material and threads. I have never tried to make a quilt but I much admire people who are able to do this.

THE CREATIVE USE OF GRIEF
by Mary Hartley
Around the time that my daughter died *my local Medway TCF group had a once a month group in a local sewing machine shop where we were making a quilt for our children. Although I'm not much of a needlewoman I had a lot of help and made a square for the quilt from some of my daughter's clothes.*

Once I'd finished that, I used to take my knitting along instead. We also had crafting days where we made scrapbook pages for our children, to go in an album, and other things like collages and candle holders.

The thing about all these activities is that, as well as engaging us in making tributes for our children, they gave us the opportunity to chat in a very relaxed atmosphere. *The ordinary group meetings are very good but this was something a little bit different and we'd often find ourselves talking more deeply and openly than we ever had before. You can see the* *same thing happening at the residential weekends, where the crafting room is the place you go to wind down when you need to, and I think it's hugely beneficial.*

***

How very special it must be to create a quilt in your child's name and to do it together:

QUILTING
by Irene Baldock
My TCF Medway group made a memory quilt back in 2007. It was a very therapeutic thing to do and we have now started another one...

Sewing Memories into a Unique Quilt
It was a real labour of love. Grieving parents or family members have united to produce an exquisite patchwork quilt. Every stitch in every square is dedicated to the memory of a loved one.

The process of holding something in your hand and sewing, concentrates the mind and thought processes on the now. *The selection of colours, materials and small items special to the child incorporated into the sewing, makes it a talking point. The elements and what they meant to each child was especially therapeutic.*

Creating the quilt has brought bereaved families together. 'We will never forget our children but meeting other people who have been through the same experiences can be very supportive.' The quilt has been displayed at exhibitions and is a focus of annual candlelight remembrance ceremonies.

MY CRAFTING JOURNEY
by Cazz Fleet

Before Tristan died, I crafted. Xmas and birthday presents for me were a doddle for Tristan. Find an online craft store that did vouchers - buy one for mum - simple.

I was taught to knit and crochet by my aunt Neno. I crocheted Tristan's dedication robe. I also used to do cross stitching. Tristan asked me once to buy him a small cross stitch kit. He chose a baseball glove holding a ball. He took the kit and a cross stitch magazine to his room and came down about 15 minutes later, having done 4 stitches and said, 'It's taking shape'. We laughed and laughed. The phrase has stuck and it is still in use today. 'It's taking shape' is the tag line for my website which I am in the process of building.

After cross stitching, I didn't do any crafts for a long while. Then I went to a class, made a greeting card and I was hooked. My crafting adventure had started again: Handmade bespoke cards, mixed media pieces, canvas art works, decorative boxes, etc etc etc.

Simple jewellery making followed and then I got a sewing machine. My last attempt at sewing had been a failed attempt to make a skirt at school. **But I followed the KISS method - Keep It Simple, Stupid.** Bag after bag after bag rolled under the needle. Family and friends eagerly took care of them and I sold a lot too.

Then Tristan died... Everything came to a halt. I had no desire to make or create anything. Dust began to cover my machine, craft tools, paper, fabric... everything. What was the point anymore? I would sit looking at all my craft stash. One day I decided I was going to get rid of it all and started to think about how to do it. I dozed in my chair and a voice as clear as *a bell said to me, 'Don't you dare sell any of it mum, I paid for most of it,' and I heard Tristan's laugh at the end of it.*

Slowly, slowly, I would create something - even it was just a small fabric flower. *My creativity was slowly coming back. I got into digital design and printed up a pile of cards that I now sell at a chiropractic clinic where I work and all the profits go to TCF. I plan to have some of my designs printed professionally to sell on my website, again with all profits going to TCF.*

Crafting, whatever it may be, helps me to block out reality just for a short while. It's calming, therapeutic and relaxing. I couldn't be without it now.

WHEN I WANT A HUG…
by Anne Morgan, TCF Victoria, Australia
Remembering my son, Darren, and his partner, Carol, who died in a car accident
It took four years for me to realise he wouldn't be coming home again. I got all his clothes out and made a quilt from his shirts and jeans, even though there were holes from welding flares and oil marks that wouldn't come out. From his singlets I made hearts and butterflies and all the buttons from his shirts (196) were sewn into the corners of the squares.

I put a piece in the middle and wrote what happened to them both, and when, and how proud we are to have had such a loving son… **When I want a hug from my son I wrap the quilt around me.** *It is nowhere near the same, but it helps. We have it on our bed, or over a chair, and wherever it is, Darren is with us.*

ART THERAPY
by Lauren Foster
About six months after my son, Rex, died, I joined an art therapy group. *This group gave me something to do when I*

didn't know what to do with myself. I learnt how to needle felt, then went home, purchased a needle and some wool, and started creating!

Felting appealed to me and it helped me to get some relief from the thoughts that were forever swirling around in my head. **I was doing something positive, and I felt OK when I was doing it.**

My art therapy group had people in it that had been through a similar life experience to me. We created a large felted piece together, it was an amazing experience. A part of every person in that group was in the art, we felt connected to each other, part of something bigger than ourselves.

I decided to study and become an art therapist. Art helped me to get through the days and has now excited me about the future where at one time I didn't believe I could be excited about anything ever again. I know now that I don't have to have any artistic skills to create. Everyone can create.

Bringing Art therapy to TCF has been something I have wanted to do since I started to study. I knew that like me there would be others who might benefit from it in some way. So the 'Express Yourself Through Art' group was formed.

The group has participated in many art processes which support them in exploring aspects of their lives. Using different materials and processes each month, participants have been able to **give their thoughts a break and immerse themselves in the doing of the art.**

They don't need to create aesthetically pleasing art work. The participants formed their own insights from their work, talking about it with others, or taking notice of how it was for them when creating it.

The group have created personal art pieces and pieces together. Last month, the group created a mural on the outside wall at the Texas Council on Family Violence Centre. An amazing garden emerged. It was a wonderful experience to be part of.

I am proud of and grateful to the courageous participants. They all worked generously together, accommodating each other's needs, making sure everyone felt they had done what they needed to do. Hopefully when people drop by, they can have a look at the mural, know that it has been created by parents and siblings who share similar experiences, and feel a connection to it.

NEW HOBBIES

I've just bought myself a jigsaw. So many people have told me how sitting down, forgetting all the jobs piling up, and trying to solve a jigsaw puzzle gives them a much needed space. For a while their mind can have a rest from all those thoughts and emotions overtaking them as they try to fit all those odd shapes and colours together.

My new jigsaw is an attractive countryside scene with a pond, ducks, a kingfisher, otter and many brightly coloured flowers. I'd better sit at the table to do it except that I love my armchair. I think I've got a large board somewhere... Found it, and yes, I'm starting by sifting out all the pieces with edges; that feels like an ordered thing to do, which is quite unlike me.

Right I've got the frame together. It's time for a cup of tea. I put the board with all its pieces on the table. It's there, I can go back to it whenever...

As I'm putting the kettle on and fishing out the milk from the fridge I remember the poem about jigsaws which was read out during the candle lighting at one of our residential weekends. It's a poem written for bereaved families of Ontario by Victoria Guthrie:

Grief is like a Jigsaw Puzzle
by Victoria Guthrie

Grief is not a smorgasbord where you go down the line picking a little of this and a little of that.

Grief is like a jigsaw puzzle. Some people get all the edge pieces together first and work from the outside in.

Others dump everything out on the table at once and jump right into the middle.

Some never open the box at all. They just look at the picture on the outside and wonder why what's inside the box doesn't match or make sense.

You meet a lot of people when you start a jigsaw puzzle. Some are full of advice or they may try to make the puzzle look the way it ought to be instead of the way it is.

But, once in awhile, you meet someone who shares their own finished puzzle and helps you to make some sense of yours.

Then you find it is not as hard as before. Some of the pieces fit together more easily, and you sigh with relief...and remember.

***

Yoga is not for everyone but I sometimes do a session with my friend who is a Dru Yoga teacher. We concentrate on exercises which strengthen the muscles in my chest and do breathing exercises as I have lung problems. At the end I am breathing more easily and because of this I feel much calmer and more relaxed. Margot Smith has found it helps her face life in a more positive way rather than as a powerless victim.

YOGA FOR HEALING
by Margot Smith, (Georgia's mum)
I had all the classic signs and symptoms of someone who was experiencing trauma and loss. I felt isolated and separate from the world, and constantly experienced the emotions of fear, anger and guilt. I faced each day with dread and deep sadness. Others in my first yoga class were unaware of my suffering because emotional paralysis is not as obvious as physical paralysis.

The yoga class was a place to feel nurtured, safe and honoured for the human-being-ness and not doing-ness. It was also a place to go beyond the superficial or material world. I was now searching for answers to 'life's purpose'.

I discovered the yoga teachings from class could be incorporated into daily life and assisted with building inner strength and courage like a self-help prescription for my heart.

After a traumatic event such as the death of a child, the fight and flight mechanism can be constantly activated, adrenaline levels are high which deletes our energy and maintains high stress levels. Many of the yoga sequences and relaxations helped initiate the relaxation response. I became less stressed and my ability to cope improved.

Breath awareness techniques helped with flashbacks and challenges such as anniversaries by bringing me into the present moment.

I live and breathe yoga because I have experienced the benefits and the shift from negative patterns to positive ones. Relationships have improved and the qualities of fear, insecurity and anger have been replace with courage, trust, forgiveness, acceptance and gratitude.

I now teach three classes a week and this in itself has helped me move from a powerless victim to discover an inner power that enables me to give back to others. I live life in a way that honours Georgia and the precious gift life is. To come from such a dark place and then to help add value to other people's lives is a gift.

Sometimes the most tragic events can become the biggest catalyst for awakening even if it is not wanted at the time, and yoga has been a wonderful vehicle for the journey of 'healing and growing'.

***

Whatever we find to do that absorbs us and gives us precious moments free from the all absorbing grief is valuable beyond words.

BELL RINGING
by Patsy Glover

I have begun to learn to bell ring since Evie died. I go with another bereaved mother, Jane, to the church in Bath where the celebration for Evie's life was held. I am not musical - I haven't played an instrument since the age of 11 when I learned the violin. Evie was the musical one in the family - she played the saxophone.

However, I go each week and practice. For that hour I am totally absorbed in the sound of my bell, pulling the rope with just the right amount of strength and trying to fit in with the other bell ringers. I laugh; sometimes Jane and I cry afterwards as we talk about our children. Bell ringing is a much needed distraction!

CIRCLE DANCING
by Jan Davies

I started a new interest in 2003 - Circle Dancing. I remember vividly my first evening: I enjoyed the dancing immensely throughout. When we reached the last dance, the lights were turned off, and we danced with the flickering candles of the centrepiece. It was magical, and I had a strange feeling that I had danced the dance before in a previous life.

A few weeks later, we had a jolly sailors' dance with rocking movements. I kept rocking the wrong way and bumping into the person next to me. We both started laughing, and the tears dripped down my face. On the way home, I realised that I had not laughed so unrestrainedly since our younger son died seven years before. It was such a release.

Now I run a group, and firmly believe in the therapeutic power of Circle Dancing.

PLAYING THE KEYBOARD
by Dorothy Kelly

We lost our precious 21 year old daughter, Alison, in 2009. Knowing we would never part with her keyboard, a few years later I thought I could maybe make use of it. Never having touched a musical instrument before I enquired about lessons: it was all very daunting for me but I persevered and still take lessons.

I amazed myself by passing Grade 1 piano exam. It's a closeness to Alison and it feels like she's putting my fingers on the right keys.

RESEARCHING THE FAMILY TREE
by Mary Hartley

After about five years, my grief, although still very painful, was becoming easier. I was re-engaging with life but there was still a huge gap and I felt the need to 'do something' to occupy myself but couldn't summon up much enthusiasm for anything. Then my nephew started to research one branch of the family tree and, to our huge surprise, we found our East End family actually hailed from rural Oxfordshire, a little town called Watlington.

I went with my nephew, and a niece, to look at the place, visit the local records office and 'walk where they'd walked' and I was hooked on genealogy.

Nowadays I have about 2500 people on my own family tree, and have researched several other people's families for them. I've connected with relations from across the globe, have found so many interesting, and often naughty, stories and have found hours have flown by while I've been trawling through records online or in a dusty old archive.

It's also been poignant for me to find out how many of my ancestors, and even my aunts and uncles, have been bereaved parents. Up until around the 1930s it was more unusual to have died before all of your children than to have outlived any of them and you can find evidence in surviving documents of the way people supported each other through their grief, like we support each other in TCF.

I'm not suggesting that everybody starts researching their family tree but, as time goes by, I think it is helpful to find something that really interests you, and engages your mind, be it gardening, painting, writing or whatever. My next step is to start writing the stories of some of my ancestors' lives and, to that end, I've enrolled on a creative writing course. I still miss my daughter every day but I do find my hobby is making it easier to get through the days and even to enjoy my life.

***

Now this gives me an idea. Thank you Mary. I am half Welsh and was brought up in Swansea, South Wales. My great grandfather was a well known writer and orator. Lloyd George popped in to have tea with him once and I've got a cup and saucer from that tea service at home - *Sorry, I had to put that bit in!* I would love to know more about this branch of my family. So...

UKO AGAIN!

HOW IT IS FOR ME
by Anne Bray

It was good to read the magazine, Compassion, today. I also received a parcel of library books from Mary, so I'm feeling very blessed by TCF.

What helps me? Looking after myself, trying to do what feels possible, and being ok with leaving what doesn't! Easier said than done, I know, and I'm fortunate that I'm not working, and live alone, so can do what I choose when I choose, even if lonely at times.

I made a list of 10 points headed Look After Yourself. Different points have helped me on hard days and easier days, and I look at the list often to remind myself.

> **Look After Myself**
> Celebrate small things
> Celebrate big things
> Don't compare
> Make time for exercise
> Eat well
> Look for the good
> Stop being so hard on yourself
> Have some rest. And don't feel guilty about it
> Give yourself a pat on the back
> Bed early

I find that when I feel better I try to do more than I have energy for, don't look after myself so well and then take a dip. I guess this is what happens to us all, but the list helps me get back on track. Bereavement requires a great deal of time and patience.

Different activities help at different times. Reading a book was hard for a long time, owing to lack of concentration, but quotations and reading others' stories helped me, reminding me it's not just me. Looking at photos is sometimes a joy and other times just not possible, but when I felt I was able to, I put together a special collection.

How do I cope with anniversaries? It's hard. As soon as I'm through one, I get anxious about the next one! I'm sure that making some sort of plan for the day is helpful, and when it arrives it can be easier than expected. It's only nine months since Jess died, so very early days, but my husband died nine years ago so I'm remembering the early years of that bereavement too.

A lot has been said and written about friends and how they can be helpful or not. I find that a good listener, with concern and compassion for me, who I can meet with regularly, is very important to my wellbeing.

Being at the TCF residential weekend at Ammerdown in Somerset and meeting everyone was a great support. There were so many different elements that were helpful. I will share a particularly poignant moment. When we gathered to remember our children at the Candle Lighting on Saturday evening, the music played was Spiegel im Spiegel by Arvo Pärt. Jess was an accomplished violinist, and played that piece at her brother's wedding. It was difficult to listen to and to know that I will never hear her play again, but it reminded me of a very happy day we spent together.

Writing this reminds me of another of my primary strategies when difficult emotions well up. I allow the tears to flow, but also then let my thoughts turn from sadness to thanks. So for me, being grateful gives me strength.

That's how it is for me!

WHAT KEPT ME SANE
by Marcia Thompson

Our son was diagnosed with an incurable brain tumour in April 2016 and that's when our grieving started. In some ways, this was a more difficult time for us than when he died. He stayed more or less OK for a couple of years, but the last months were very hard as he deteriorated rapidly and needed our care.

It was physically and emotionally hard. I think this is different from a sudden death. A lot of grieving is done at diagnosis. When we see our children suffering so much, and know they will not get better, I have no problem in saying, we wanted it to end. And when it does end, it is terrible. Because we always hope there might be a miracle. When our son died we had feelings of Grief, Disbelief and Relief.

So, what kept me sane? What kept me going?

It is important to be able to get up in the morning and to have something to get up for. *For me, these have been various:*

I started doing Jigsaws and was keen to make progress.
I knitted and was keen to add a few rows.
I had made arrangements with friends and needed to be available.

Walking is essential. Being out in the fresh air was so helpful. And if you are walking with a group, they don't mind if you're on your own at times, if you don't feel sociable. Conversely, a social occasion is hard as I feel people are looking at me to see how I'm coping.

I like gardening. Mindless exercise. I do think a lot and cry, but I have achieved something, even if it's just brushing up a few leaves. And achieving something is so helpful.

I gave up some of my activities. I've always loved music but find it too emotional at the moment, though am trying to wean myself back on to it.

I've started a textile class which is a new venture. Everyone is friendly. They are a lot better than I am, but I accept the fact that I am a newcomer and am pleased with the small successes I have made.

I have gone to Quaker meetings. That silence is very helpful. No-one expects anything of me.

I have had periods of depression in my life and have almost gone under. Now, faced with something a million times worse, I am coping. I think perhaps the way my son, Matthew, coped with his devastating illness, has helped me to cope with my loss.

WHAT HELPS ME
by Helen Asbury

My 31 year old son took his life five years ago, after an almost lifelong struggle with depression and self esteem. I had thought he was at last doing well, so it was an immense shock. In the immediate aftermath, I think four things kept me from following him:

My other son and my daughter - knowing I must not compound their grief by dying too, knowing that they needed to be assured of my love and support for them, that my love for their brother was not more important to me than my love for them.

My work - I was a psychotherapist, and working at a deep level with others struggling with their difficult lives was a respite from my own grief, and for a while, I believe, my own recent experience enabled me to do deep work, engaging with clients in a way I could not previously have done. I burned out after a couple of years or so, and realised I needed to take a break for my clients' sake and my own.

My therapist, *with whom I had built a deep professional relationship over many years as support for my work, was an absolute life-saver. I could talk to her about what had happened, and how I was feeling.*

Friends *who gently cared for me, enticed me out and back into my social group early on, and who I knew were there for me, even when they stopped asking all the time how I was doing.*

Now, five years down the line, I have retired, and last year moved away from my lifelong home area and friends, to live next door to my daughter in another city. Moving to a completely new area has been a challenge, but I am determined not to be a burden on my daughter, so have pushed myself out of my comfort zone and made myself meet new people and make a life of my own here.

I sleep badly and when my eyes are too tired to read, I listen to Radio 4 or the World Service. Background sound helps me drop off to sleep.

I play tennis, and joining a club gives me exercise and a social life, both of which I find profoundly helpful in combatting my natural tendency to turn inward and fester. Often I don't want to go to tennis, but I almost always feel better when I do. It's early days, and I know it takes time to build true friendships, but just forcing myself to take an interest in others really helps make me feel better.

I feel I must live as best I can for as long as I naturally have, keeping busy and spending time with other people. I would like to think that at some point in the future I could pick up my professional experience and use it in some form of support for other bereaved parents.

JOINING CLASSES
by Ruby Green
I lost my lovely daughter, Siân, in 1985 aged 20. She died from suicide after years of mental suffering.

A few weeks after she died, I forced myself to join a calligraphy class which enabled me to forget my turmoil for a while. It is a discipline which requires a lot of concentration and accuracy to get a satisfactory result. After my husband died in 1996, I joined a class in reflexology which was very therapeutic as also was gardening.

Then after a few months, TCF came into my life through a TCF programme, and I was befriended by County Contact, Rita Henshaw, and other bereaved parents, and they are still my dearest friends.

WHAT FEEDS MY SOUL
by Claire Phillips
We lost our daughter Lucy in 2000. She was 15 years old and she died from a seizure as she had been diagnosed with epilepsy when she was 10. We didn't know that people could die from seizures and since then we have been involved with an epilepsy charity (SUDEP Action) which researches into this. SUDEP means Sudden Unexpected Death from Epilepsy. This has also helped us a lot. Mark my husband is a trustee for the charity and meeting other people bereaved by epilepsy has helped as well as feeling that we are contributing something to make the situation better.

I find that the WEA (Workers Education Association) classes in literature help to keep me focused. Besides being with other people, it involves learning new things combined with directed reading. Often the issues in novels and poetry involve loss and dealing with the aftermath. I did a study day on John Clare recently and came out inspired. He wrote about loss and isolation, and he wrote poems about his children and the children that had died. This feeds my soul!

WHAT HELPS?
by Liz Farmilo

The dog - he is the same all the time - he's not been affected by our loss and still wants to go for a walk, be fed and have company and is always, always pleased to see us!

Being in beautiful natural landscapes - very early on we went to spend time just looking at beautiful countryside near us and it was soothing.

Meeting others who have experienced losing a child. I didn't know how true that saying is, that your address book will change - mine has a LOT of bereaved mums in it now! I have a particular friend who lost a daughter a few months after we lost our son and we meet up every couple of months or so and it is SO healing.

Fundraising and charity work - I have organised a Hope Walk for Papyrus for the last two years. I make filled rolls for my local pub's quiz night in exchange for donations to them too. I have become an area contact and started a support group for TCF. Helping others helps me.

Working less - although this was on the cards before Stephen died, it helps me to have the time to be able to just do nothing sometimes, to acknowledge my grief and to spend time thinking about Stephen.

Friends and family - seeing more of these important people in my life and making more effort to do so as I now REALLY appreciate just how important they are!

Therapy - I found myself bursting to talk to someone neutral a few months after Stephen's death. I went to see a psychotherapist for about a year and it really helped me understand my grief more, and to give myself permission to handle it the way I need to and not to worry about pleasing anyone else. It's also given me the confidence to express my feelings much better.

Laughter - retaining a sense of humour has been essential.

Making photo montages to hang up round our house and sorting out the childhood drawings, videos and photos has been therapeutic - somehow it makes me feel a bit better that these are now more organised so I can look at them when I want. I had no idea how precious they would become!

***

If you're searching for something to do that can help you, I hope that reading about what helps others will give you a few ideas, and that eventually, you will find an activity that helps you through your grief.

HOW TCF BEGAN

How did The Compassionate Friends start…? It all began in Coventry Hospital where two sets of parents were visiting their sons, each in different wards. One boy had cancer and the other had suffered a serious road accident.

A young chaplain, Simon Stephens, was helping both families and introduced them to each other. He, himself, had been bereaved through a fatal car accident…

Here are the stories told by two of the founders.

LEGACY OF LOVE
by Simon Stephens

Who was I angry with all those years ago? Angry with God. If God was almighty, surely he could control the situation. Why did he permit a drunken driver to mow through the family car? Surely somewhere along the line he could have made the lorry driver drive into a ditch, why did he choose that road and our car?

Then I was angry with the emergency and medical services. Surely they could have saved at least one life apart from mine. And what about the lorry driver? If I could have killed him I would have. The courts sentenced him to two years imprisonment, six months for each life, which was reduced on appeal to three months. I saw him 14 months later in an Esso tanker driving through our town. So anger was a major problem in my life. Then I moved on, still nursing my anger, to guilt. I wonder how many of you find that guilt is squeezing your heart?

Guilt, because my parents did not wish to go to that meeting. 'We don't want to go, Simon.' My mother was a French nursing sister and had had a heavy day on the wards. My father had had a busy day and wanted to work in the garden. The evenings were getting lighter; rhododendrons were out; spring was in the air. But I said, 'We've got to go otherwise we shall not be accepted for our grades for university next year'. So I almost opened the car's door and pushed my family in and within half an hour of doing that, four of them were dead. So guilt certainly squeezed my heart as much as anger.

Initially, after I buried my family, I had a great chip on my shoulder. I was a thoroughly unpleasant person. Nobody wanted to know me. The educator said, 'Grow up and forget'; the parish clergy said, 'Say your prayers and you'll be fine'. I wanted to climb to the top of a mountain and scream my family's names, but I was denied that and told to 'carry on'.

Grief is a very powerful emotion in our lives. It is the price we pay for love. *I loved my family dearly and always will; they always play a major role in my life - but I believe that if we can exorcise from our hearts anger and guilt then the crown of thorns which is unresolved grief becomes the victor's laurels.*

The loveliest people I've ever met have been men and women who've been to hell and back again because they have buried their dearly loved children and have found comfort and strength in TCF. They've been able to put their hands out in the darkness to others who are lost in the deep darkness of that valley.

I also believe that grief can be creative. When we begin to do the hard work of grieving. My doctor said, 'Simon, Valium will help. There's no need for you to cry - take Valium'. But we all know that when we are walking through the Valley of the Shadow, when we shed our tears, we are purging the wound of grief and we are beginning to find an area of healing in our lives. So as we go through our valley, we consider our anger, what we are doing with it or what it is doing to us.

I suspect that many of us have said to ourselves, 'We could have prevented the death from taking place. If we had done this, done that, those whom we love would be with us now'. Some of us, when we think like this, never move on to the next step in the valley, and if we don't, we will never see the butterflies dancing on the valley's rim. We have to move forward. But many of us can only do that when TCF is holding us by the hand.

Anger, guilt, disbelief, rehabilitation. Some professionals say, 'Simon, grief is six weeks long and if after six weeks people are still grieving, then they need to see a psychiatrist'. But each one of us has a different valley to walk and for some the valley is life-long, while for some it is a much shorter distance. But we do not have to walk alone in that valley. As our creed states, 'We do not walk alone; we are The Compassionate Friends; we walk together'.

How do we enter the process of rehabilitation? Well, I believe in the 'Legacy of Love'. Your greatest gift from your child is the gift of love. Love is immortal, love is eternal, love is not a passive force within our lives. We can transform this world of ours, which is often so sick and sad, with the gift of love the children have given us.

What are you doing with your child's legacy of love? TCF world-wide has taught me that the legacy of love is being put to good use. I've been greatly humbled and heartened travelling the world as I do, whenever the Navy says I can, that bereaved parents, instead of holding their child's love and clasping it to their hearts, have opened their hands, taken the legacy of love and shared it with parents who are walking through the valley of the shadow.

We all have tremendous potential. I know from my own experience when I buried my family that for a long time nobody wanted to know me. I was an emotional cripple in so many ways. I was so bitter and twisted. But the community in which I eventually found myself in Africa took me to one side, sat me down and for the first time, 18 months later, let me talk through my anger and guilt and they let me shed my tears.

Are you stuck on stage one? 'God why me… Why the church… Why did the world…Why did medicine fail my child? Are you angry with the person who took your child's life, or have you moved on perhaps one step and find yourself looking at guilt in your life? Every time you see an empty chair or a photograph, do you find them an indictment? Have you moved on beyond your guilt? And if you've moved on beyond both, have you come to terms with your child's death? And have you begun to invest their legacy of love? When did you last see butterflies at the end of the valley?

Every day of my life I talk to my family. When I was anchored in Sydney harbour, I went up in the early hours of the morning to get some fresh air from the smells of a naval ship. A sailor found me talking to my family on the flight deck and said, 'Padre, are you OK?' and I said, 'I'm talking to my family'. He looked astonished and I said, 'They are with us here this morning'. Do you talk to those you have lost? If you do, you're well on the road to rehabilitation and acceptance. Do you discuss with them all the major decisions you make? Certainly before I joined the Royal Navy I said to my family, 'Do you know where I'm going next? I'm going to join the Royal Navy!' and I'm sure they were as amazed as I.

You know the church has some marvellous phrases - 'the

whole company of heaven', 'the whole crowd of witnesses'. **Our children are with us; the legacy of love, which our children have given today, is given so we may transform tomorrow. Our children have an active role in our lives. And we betray them, without any doubt, if we do not invest that love in the coming years.**

I have been humbled beyond measure by my wandering around TCF world-wide. I have met people whose hearts have been broken, whose marriages have fallen apart, people who have on their hearts suicide attempts - and yet they have been able to work through their guilt and through their anger. They realise their children are with them and they have made a significant contribution to the beauty of the world in which we live.

The Compassionate Friends, world-wide, is a monument to our children. *We represent every race, every culture and every colour. In Africa I went to a mud hut on the shores of Lake Victoria and there was a TCF logo stuck on the mud door. We are a large family and I believe that together we can make it, for their sake.*

***

OUR STORY
by Joe Lawley
The family was engaged in the usual early morning hassle as we washed, dressed, ate and finally shared a moment as the children left for school. We were four: Iris and Joe, parents, Angela (the elder of our children, aged nearly fifteen) and Kenneth, the younger, nearly twelve. The youngsters departed and then, minutes later, as we prepared to leave too, the telephone rang. I picked it up, a voice said, 'There's been an accident. Kenneth has been taken to hospital by ambulance.'

We rushed to the hospital convincing each other that it could be nothing worse than a broken limb, but within a short time we knew that it was serious, he was unconscious; later we were told that he had suffered major head injuries, with resultant brain damage. We were face-to-face with death.

Elsewhere in the hospital was another boy, Billy Henderson, suffering from cancer. His parents had nursed him through a long illness, at his bedside day and night. We discovered later that the Henderson family (Bill and Joan, the parents, Andrew and Billy, their sons, and daughters, Shona and Susan) and ourselves were all known to the Rev. David Dale, a minister in the United Reformed Church.

Standing back from the constant group of relatives and friends round Kenneth's bed in the Intensive Care Unit was another young man in clerical garb, the Reverend Simon Stephens. He simply said, 'If I can help....I am here, all of the time.' Eventually we asked, 'Will you pray for Kenneth?' and when he did so, he mentioned Billy Henderson. Thus we came to know somewhere in this vast hospital another boy lay dying, another family hoped and prayed.

It was not to be. Kenneth died on 23rd May 1968 - a day now indelibly stamped in our memory. Billy Henderson died a few days later. Iris suggested that we send flowers to Joan and Bill; we did not then know the significance of that act, but looking back, it might be said that The Compassionate Friends started there. Joan and Bill telephoned their thanks and we met for a cup of tea. Together, midst freely flowing tears, the four of us were able for the first time to speak openly of our children, without feelings of guilt that we were endlessly repeating the virtues of our children, and of our vanished hopes for the future.

Together, we were all able to accept, for the first time, the words used by many well-meaning friends - rejected almost universally by parents who have lost a beloved child -'I understand'. We did understand, all four of us, and, in the immensity of our grief (and in reality is there any other tragedy of quite this enormity?), we all suffered together.

We were helping each other - a telephone call in the blackest hour brought love and help immediately to the door; the regular family visits, where the younger members reminded us constantly of their needs and dragged us back to the role of parent, and where the occasionally humorous incidents induced the first smiles, and even laughs - all these played their part in our journey through the experience of overwhelming grief. We were learning to live a little again. It did not happen overnight, nor even with years but it had started.

Simon Stephens, who had kept close contact with us, spotted it first. He said, 'You are helping each other in a way which I, and virtually everyone else, am unable to do, because of your shared experience; do you think it could work with other bereaved parents?' We put it to the test. We wrote to, and subsequently visited, a West Indian family who had lost a young child in a road accident. It worked. We became friends.

Simon then suggested a meeting of a number of recently bereaved parents, and the initial coming together took place January 28, 1969, in a room at the Coventry and Warwickshire Hospital, a place with poignant memories for most of us; returning to the hospital itself was, you might say, a hurdle which we needed to surmount.

In the event, six people were present - Bill and Joan Henderson, Betty Rattigan, Simon Stephens, Iris and myself. We talked about an organisation which would try to help other bereaved parents. But the number of child deaths in the UK was dauntingly large - would we be able to cope with what might become an overwhelming demand for our time. We decided to try.

What about a name? The word 'compassion' had featured frequently in our conversation, and eventually 'The Society of the Compassionate Friends' emerged. It sounded right then, and now in a slightly shorter form, it still sounds right - perhaps even inspired.

To round off this part of the history of The Compassionate Friends, I would like to record the names of that first committee. They were: Honorary President - Simon Stephens; Chairman - Joe Lawley; Secretary - Betty Rattigan; Coordinator - Joan Henderson; Treasurer - Bill Henderson; Member and Visitor - Iris Lawley.

***

And so 'The Compassionate Friends' was born. Iris and Joe Lawley, Joan and Bill Henderson, and Betty Rattigan continued to visit bereaved parents as soon as they heard of the death of a child. As time went by there began to be too many to visit individually, so group support meetings were started.

As TCF grew, the group meetings and other means of support expanded to the whole country and eventually abroad. The organisation of The Compassionate Friends is now established in 30 countries, comforting and supporting bereaved parents, grandparents and siblings - thanks to those six bereaved people who got together in a room at the Coventry and Warwickshire hospital, and decided to make a difference.

TCF GROUP SUPPORT MEETINGS

RELEASE
I was terrified I'd break down
I did
It didn't matter
Rosalind M Baker

THE COMPASSIONATE FRIENDS hold group support meetings monthly and sometimes fortnightly, They are all run by bereaved parents. My friend, Sue Hughes, whose son, Joe, died ten years ago, holds one at her home in Marlow and I go and help her when I can.

We are welcomed by a hug and a cup of tea or coffee and then we sit down and chat. It all tumbles out, our despair, our tears, our stories, our grief… And amidst that, happy memories of our children, rays of hope that it will not always be like this…

NO LONGER ALONE
by Lindsey D'Olier
As a fairly newly bereaved parent I was at a complete loss with my grief. I was lucky to find TCF very early on. I have met some amazingly strong women who, without any words, completely understand my torment. When I know of our next monthly meeting I almost gallop to the gathering, to a safe haven of 'people like me.'

The mothers I have met have managed to fill me with hope that I too will someday find that joy and ability to 'live' that they now seem to have years down the road.

I have met new friends through TCF that otherwise I would not have met, and we share something no one in my previous life could possibly understand. This is invaluable to me. I am no longer alone on this journey.

***

I went to a meeting the first time to cry.
I went back the second time to be heard.
I went back the third time to start to heal
and help someone else who was there
for the first time.

Jack,
TCF, Salem, Oregon Chapter

THANK YOU TCF
by Jane Pickard

I discovered TCF in the very early days of my loss - just a few weeks after my son, Ben, died. I was desperate to connect with other grieving mothers. Even so, I dithered and hesitated for a while before stepping over the threshold and into this club, to which none of us wish to belong. But we do belong. And I am so glad that I found you - all of you who share the knowledge and pain of terrible and catastrophic loss. Because you understand. And because no one else does.

Within the group, I felt immense comfort in the knowledge that I wasn't the only one, the one to be avoided in case my child's death is somehow contagious.

Our group allows us to talk or not, to cry, to howl, to rage. And also to be still and calm, to listen to others' stories and to hold each other and our beloved children close in our hearts. To give our grief a voice. To give our children their voices and not to have people turn away when we try to talk about them.

I don't want to belong, but I do.

And I'm so glad I found you.

***

OUR VOLUNTEERS not only run the group supporting and comforting the newly bereaved; they are living proof that not only is it possible to survive, but be able to lead a full life again - a different life, but life nevertheless.

ANDREW'S STORY

A MAN'S JOURNEY TO TCF AND BEYOND
by Andrew Miller QC
When I was 12 years old, the band, 10cc, launched their most famous song, 'I'm not in love'. Those of you old enough will remember that it was a huge hit. At the time I was not old enough to understand or even try to understand the lyrics, especially given that it was about a man claiming to 'not' be in love. But I do recall the most famous words very well. They were said or sung as a whisper… 'Big boys don't cry, big boys don't cry.' To a 12 year old boy that seemed a very sensible statement. Only babies and young children and maybe older girls cry… but certainly, big boys do not cry. That was in 1975.

Little did I know that some 40 years later in 2015 I would discover just how much a 'big boy' could cry, when I lost my own little boy, my dearest Fabian. *Fabian was only 19 years old. This fact is nothing new to any bereaved parent. The tears, that you never knew were there, come from nowhere and seem to be endless. It does not matter who you are, a mum, a dad, a sibling or grandparent, those tears come and yes, 'big boys do cry'.*

But in the case of men, those tears often stop or are consciously stopped all too soon. Because in the end men are not supposed to cry, not supposed to show their feelings, not supposed to be the emotional one. This often appears to be the general belief that abounds. But no one made those rules and even if they did, it is unlikely that they had ever lost a child.

And so I was one of those men. Not quite sure how I should be reacting, what I should be doing or saying, how I should be behaving with my family, with my friends, with my work colleagues and with the world in general. It was in fact a woman, now my dearest Esther, who found TCF for me.

There was no group local to me but one not too far in Finchley, North London. I made contact with the wonderful Pat who runs it, found out the details and on the first Tuesday in June of 2015, some five months since losing Fabian, I found myself driving to my first meeting. I managed to convince myself that I would actually be turned away. 'No... you have made a mistake... this is a group for bereaved parents... not for you.' How wrong or delusional could I have been. **I was, of course, welcomed with open and hugging arms. I was told I was in the right place, a safe place, a place where I was meant to be.** And so I stayed.

And what did I notice first thing? There were 18 in the group. A large group but only four men. I was told that it was a good turnout for men that week. Sometimes they had only one or two and many times, no men at all. Apparently, that was normal... men did not engage as much with TCF as women. All to do with the emotions or lack of them, or the inability to show them. It was all a bit confusing. Anyway, I sat down in this sea of bereaved parents and a couple of siblings. I sat, I listened, I shed a tear and I got to tell my story.

That meeting changed everything about my grief journey. *Many users of TCF talk about how meeting other bereaved parents was their saving moment... their life line. It was the same for me. Something happened at that meeting that sent me on a new path. In the past five months I felt that I understood what it was like to lose a child. In my naivety when I entered the room, the one thing I had assumed was that we were all on the same wavelength or understanding.*

As I sat there listening to the many stories being told by so *many parents, about their child and their loss, my naive thought was shattered. I had lost Fabian to drugs. I had some understanding of that loss, how it happened, what is was like going through the process, how terrible it was to find him on that tragic day.*

But I had no comprehension of what these other parents had been through. I had no idea what it was like to lose a child to cancer, or a road accident or to medical malpractice or to suicide or to a freak accident. I knew only my loss. I had no idea of what they had been through, how they had reacted and how they were coping. But it showed me or made me realise something so very important. I remember distinctly listening to one parent describe how she had lost her beautiful ten year old daughter to cancer. She told her story and that of her daughter with such dignity, such courage, such tenderness and with such grief.

*What struck me was the effect that hearing that story (and all the others) had on me and everyone else there. When a parent had finished their tragic story, no other parent or sibling could ever say (or ever wanted to say)… 'Well you think that is bad… what about me?' That was impossible. **Every story was a tragedy, every story was a loss that should not have been.** And therefore every story had an ability to disarm you as a fellow bereaved parent, to make you realise that you were NOT ALONE in this loss and most importantly that YOU WERE NOT A VICTIM. Any victim mentality I had built up in those first five months disappeared, or at least started to disappear, at my first encounter with other bereaved parents.*

And what was the secret to all this? For me it was the realisation that for all of us, what had brought us to be sitting together in this TCF support group, was the cause of our child's or sibling's death. But what kept us together and bonded us and made us able to rely on each other was not the cause of the death, but our joint loss of a child. Very quickly I realised that it was all about the loss of our children. For me, the loss is far more significant than the cause of Fabian's death.

That first meeting was some four years ago. By some unexplainable route I found myself becoming involved as a trustee of TCF just over three and a half years ago. After about two years of losing Fabian, I was working as a volunteer at TCF weekends and now, with the incredible help of others, I run the NW/Central London group which has been going for one year and has a strong following. At our residential weekends, I take the Men's group.

The Men's group is very different from all other support and discussion groups. Firstly, there are no 'Women-only' groups. So why the need for a male only group? Well it goes back to the very beginning…'Big boys don't cry'. **Even in these modern times men and women deal with the loss of their child or sibling in different ways.** *When I take the group, I seek to run through the possible differences that they may have noticed, if they are in a marriage or partnership. How and why has it been different? There can be many and varied answers to this, but often, there is SILENCE.*

I have seen that men do not always realise that they are dealing with their grief in a different way to their wife or partner, or do not think of it as being anything out of the normal. But what does tend to be a constant in the Men's group, is how men initially react to being asked to talk about how they are doing generally, since the loss of their child. There is more often than not one of two responses to this question. The first is an avoidance of the issue. **Men often do not like to talk about how they are coping. Or by contrast, men like to stress that they are fine, really fine and that they are there for the rest** *of the family.*

The groups normally follow the same pattern... at least at the beginning of the meetings. This normality that men have created, this behavioural norm is always expressed, but at some point it seems to disappear. As if by magic, the group allows or gives men permission to move away from their perceived norm, from their comfort zone, and to find both who they are and sometimes who they want to be. There comes a point in the Men's group when the men simply START TO EXPRESS THEIR FEELINGS to each other, the initial embarrassment is gone and the truth comes out. I have seen this happen each and every time and for some it is as if by magic they have been allowed to speak and be heard. But it is nothing to be surprised about and in reality it is NOT magic.

What I have seen is simply the power of TCF being the means by which people can come together and talk about their loss. *The fact that society has, at least in the past, expected or encouraged men and women to express themselves in different ways, has not changed the basic fact that **a man will grieve just as much as a woman for the loss of a child.** The Men's group therefore offers them a place to grieve and express their grief exactly as they feel it and without any judgment. The Men's group allows men who have lost a child to be just that... a man who has lost a child. There is of course no magic; it is the most normal thing in the world... but for that short time, it often feels like magic.*

I do hope that society's attitudes in respect of men and bereavement are changing, as I think they are. Men are being encouraged to be more open, to talk about their feelings and hopefully they will. Indeed over the last three years I have seen a greater engagement of men with TCF in general. The future for bereaved men being able to express themselves more openly, is *therefore promising. But whatever happens, there remains **the strong support of TCF which is equally open and available to both men and women.** And, at our weekends, there will always be the Men's group which offers bereaved men a chance to go where they have not allowed themselves to go before.*

OUR TCF RESIDENTIAL WEEKENDS

'I've learned that I still have a lot to learn.
I've learned that people will forget what you said,
people will forget what you did, but people will
never forget
how you made them feel.'
Maya Angelou

I've chosen the poem below by Irene Lee because it sums up exactly what I felt when I first went on a TCF residential weekend as a newly bereaved parent, and also how I still feel now, many years on, looking after newly bereaved parents as a member of the volunteer team.

TCF Residential Weekends

Come, join with us, they said,
And we shall welcome you with open arms.
Come, join with us, they said,
And we shall greet you with love and understanding.
We were hesitant at first,
But yes, we decided we would come,
We needed to be welcomed,
We needed to be understood,
We needed to be loved.
So we went, still hesitant,
And yes, we were welcomed,
And yes, we were understood,
And oh yes, we were loved.
But we never expected the warmth of the welcome,
Or the measure of the love and understanding that
  greeted us.
We found so many people,

We would have recognised them anywhere,
For each person reflected our own pain, our own sorrow.
Each person had their own story to tell,
And we listened, as they listened to ours.
We cried with each other
And we laughed with each other.
There was no shame in crying,
No guilt in laughing,
There was no pretence,
Our very souls were laid bare for all to see,
And we were proud.
Proud of our children who had brought us here,
Proud to be part of this group of people,
This very special group of people,
Who had taken us in their midst so easily,
And had embraced us in their love.
We left with tears of farewell and, 'See you next year'.
We were drained and exhausted,
And yet, strangely revitalised and refreshed.
We shall come again next year,
And we shall say to others,
Come, join with us…..

Irene Lee

Coming to our weekends gives us all an opportunity to tell our story, to talk about our child and to listen to others.

WHAT HELPS? - Telling your story
by Friends from TCF Canada
Telling your grief story to people who care and will understand has many benefits. Each time you hear yourself going over the details that have produced such disruption in your life, a little of the shock effect is dissipated and the INTENSITY OF YOUR EMOTIONS IS DECREASED.

Your body chemistry will change, as if healing balm were being poured over your wounds, which in turn produces further positive change. This is a gentle and natural process that allows you gradually to accommodate this incredibly traumatic and distressing experience.

As you retell your story, you will gradually make the shift from your familiar, past relationship with your loved one to a new, internal relationship. That is, from a relationship where you were able to see, hear and touch that person, to one where the relationship is a feeling in your heart. 'Seeing' and 'hearing' in this new relationship are the memories that pass across the screen of your mind. YOU DO NOT NEED TO LET GO OR SAY GOOD-BYE.

Each time you are given an opportunity to tell your story, you may experience and express strong emotions. Unfortunately, it is often fear of stimulating emotions that may prevent people asking you questions that would be helpful in the long term. It isn't the TELLING of the story that causes upset, it is the story itself - the fact that someone you care about has died. You may appear to tell the same story over and over again, but when someone is really interested in listening, a little more detail may be added each time, or the story told from a different perspective.

You will learn to form a new attachment to your child, sibling or grandchild who has died and that new attachment will help to shape the new 'self' you will become in a changed world.

***

ONE OF THE MANY THINGS YOU GET AT A WEEKEND RETREAT IS **HUGS**. At our weekend at Woodbrooke for parents bereaved by suicide and substance use, Margaret Brearley sits under the tree in the car park and as soon as a car arrived she goes over to it and gives everyone a hug. She brings them into the foyer where I and other volunteers give them another hug…

HUGS
by Chris Mulligan, mother of Zac

Our hugs say, 'I'm strong - take some of my strength.' They also say, 'You can survive this - we did and we can help you to do so. You are no longer alone: we will walk this road with you.'

Hugging transfers energy and gives the person hugged an emotional lift. It is said that you need four a day for survival, eight for maintenance and twelve for growth.

Hugging, scientists say, is a form of communication because it can say things you don't have the words for. And the best part is… you usually can't give a hug without getting one.

***

On the Friday evening we have small groups where those more newly bereaved can tell their story and get to know others in their group. The group then go into dinner and sit together. As they have already begun to get to know each other, this breaks the ice and during dinner we hear them chatting and occasionally laughing These were the same people who had arrived three hours earlier, nervously and hesitantly, some of them in tears.

After dinner we have a session called 'Nuggets of Comfort and Hope'. We get together and some of us share what has helped us to get up in the morning and keep going through the day. This is one of the 'Nuggets' from our weekend for Newly Bereaved parents at Ammerdown, Somerset.

NUGGETS OF COMFORT AND HOPE
by Ruth Mercier
What Helps?

Reading books about grief and how others experienced grief and particularly how they survived the early raw pain and despair, helped me feel less alone, that I hadn't been singled out to be punished and that grief of this magnitude is survivable because others have survived. Reading about others' despair and complex feelings helped me to see I wasn't going mad, that what I was feeling was 'normal' in the circumstances. I took comfort and hope from this.

Watching quiz programmes such as Eggheads and Countdown helped because they are practical, logical programmes which anchored me a little when I felt totally overwhelmed by the emotional despair and emptiness, particularly in the late afternoon when my grief seemed to hit even harder and more intensely than at other times of the day and when I felt at times I would go mad or simply die from the pain of it all. I could rarely answer a question in the early days, but I would find myself feeling outrage and irritation at one of the regular panellists, just because of his huge ego and sheer arrogance. I think he was someone I could project much of my inner rage at. This reassured me a little that I could still feel things, even though much of the time I felt very numb and disengaged from life other than the pain of my loss.

In the first year, I went along with almost every suggestion from friends and family - going for hand massages, reiki, a coffee, a short walk, working with stones or shells, visiting a herbalist. I would tidy drawers endlessly and hoover constantly to try to drown out my thoughts. Generally, I would just keep, busy, busy, busy.

I found it a comfort and a release to cry in the shower or at the reiki sessions and in the car. In the second and third years, I chose to go out less and found it more helpful to spend time with myself and my thoughts. I felt I needed to give more time to Joel and to be with my emotions and my own personal sorrow, even though this was incredibly painful, overwhelming, frightening and desperately lonely most of the time. I was lonely wherever I was, and so being at home more helped in not having constantly to put on the mask and make polite conversation about things that didn't hold any meaning for me.

I couldn't go out in the garden for the first 18 months without wanting to come back in again after a few minutes. I struggled to see nature as a positive force because birds and flowers and life were continuing to exist and grow when my son had died. I felt I directed a lot of my anger, resentment and hurt at nature. I felt very strongly that it had let me down and that I couldn't trust it. Over time, nature has become more of a lifesaver. I still struggle with the concept of nature as a whole being a force for good and yet, whilst I can continue to feel this on the one hand, at the same time, I now find immense solace, peace, joy and gratitude in so many aspects of the natural world too.

My car was also a life-saver. Friends would always offer to pick me up and drop me home but, whilst their intentions were good, they often wouldn't pick me up on time or drop me home when I had had enough and needed to escape. I was willing to go along to many social events, but my concentration span and ability to cope with such occasions was limited and I needed to feel I could leave when I wanted to rather than being reliant on others. Very early on, I decided to drive to and from as many places as I could myself. I could then escape, close the car door and cry the whole way home because it felt contained and safe to do so - it was often a huge relief just to get behind the wheel.

I started my counselling degree in the Autumn following Joel's *death and whilst I wouldn't necessarily recommend such an intense course following the death of a child, nonetheless there were huge benefits in learning something new and where no one in the beginning knew anything about me other than what I chose to tell them. I found this very helpful because it offered me some respite from the pain of grieving, a distraction for parts of the day and a sort of re-engagement and focus in life, and certainly an opportunity to look very closely at myself and who I was as a mother and human being.*

Sometimes people say to me that I am very brave and very strong and that they couldn't imagine doing what I do. But I was where you are now and you will be where I am someday. The loss of a child or children is survivable, it is possible to smile, to laugh, to re-engage and to live again.

Like many of you, my greatest fear in the early days and my biggest stumbling block was my anxiety that, in contemplating the possibility of smiling, laughing and reengaging again, Joel would somehow be lost, that he would be forgotten whilst I carried on with life. I think all of us who are further along this road would say that this is absolutely not the case, that if it is possible, our children are even closer to us in heart and mind. I hope that this gives you all some comfort and hope.

***

ON THE SATURDAY WE HAVE MANY ACTIVITIES including discussion groups with a choice of subjects and a Speaker. Sometimes we have a walk organised or a visit to a nearby place on the Saturday afternoon or you can simply take time out to chat or have time in our Quiet Room filled with our children's photographs. There is a knitting group if you're a knitter, a creative writing group, and other workshops. We have a craft table where amongst other things you can decorate a jar for your child. In the evening we have our Candle Lighting where we light a candle in the decorated jar and remember our children together.

ON THE SUNDAY we have more discussion groups and finish with a Closing Ceremony. We encourage people to share their contact details with friends they have made so that they can keep in contact once the weekend is over.

That's a rough sketch of our residential weekends. But if you come, you don't have to join in any of this. It's totally up to you to choose what you want to do. If what you need is to sit in the lounge with a cup of coffee and chat, that's absolutely okay. There are also Friends, bereaved parents, who have trained as counsellors and are there to listen and talk with you on a one to one basis. You do whatever you choose to do.

This poem *To Honour You* is read at the end of many of our residential weekends retreats. For me, it means making a promise that I'm going to do my utmost to live life each day in the name of my children and in such a way as to honour them.

To Honour You

To honour you,
I get up every morning and take a breath.
And start another day without you in it.

To honour you,
I laugh and love with those who knew your smile and
*   the way*
your eyes twinkled with mischief and secret knowledge.

To honour you,
I take the time to appreciate everyone I love, I know now
there is no guarantee of days or hours spent in their
* presence.*

To honour you,
I listen to music you would have liked, and sing
at the top of my lungs with the windows rolled down.

To honour you,
I take chances, say what I feel, hold nothing back,
risk making a fool of myself and dance every dance.

You were my light, my heart, my gift of love
from the very highest source.

So every day I promise to make a difference,
share a smile, live, laugh and love.

Now I live for us both, so all I do,
I do to honour you.

Connie F Kiefer Byrd

I'd like to share with you some of the comments we received after one of these weekends:

'I am so grateful to have been able to attend the weekend. I have never cried so much in one weekend, and equally, I have never laughed so much! Thank you ALL'.

'You offered an experience which allowed me the peace, space and environment to share my particular agony with other bereaved parents who I know will become new friends. It was a special time, and I have left with memories of safety, warmth and security.'

'A wonderful weekend Retreat at Woodbrooke…A place where

there is no need to explain, or justify one's existence. A place just to be, to speak a very familiar language and to be understood, to make new friends, to be loved and to love in return. A great Men's group led by Andrew, listen up guys we CAN do this! Thank you all so much, my first retreat, and definitely not my last. Thank you to everyone at TCF making this such a special time of affirmation, love and celebration of our children's lives. We have been cared for so well.'

'What has sustained me the most since I left, came up in the last discussion group I attended, which was led by two facilitators quite a bit further along this path than me. They both said that, after a period of yearning for their children, and wondering where they might be, they had come to believe that their children had come back - that they now resided somewhere inside them. The idea that Emma's spirit or soul might have returned full circle to where it first began, at the centre of my being, gives me such comfort.'

***

'When you stand (or even sit) and share your story
in an empowering way,
your story will heal you
and your story will heal somebody else.'

TCF ONLINE SUPPORT

Have you thought of turning to an online group for support? There are times when we're feeling low and need to turn to someone and spill out our thoughts and feelings but nobody's around. If you're a member of a supportive online group there is always someone to listen to you..

'The comfort I've found on the TCF Forum has been the best thing. When things are especially hard I come here and write down how I feel, always getting a response and I realise I am not alone. To everybody at TCF, Thank You.'

Vera

We have a very active online peer to peer support including an online Forum and several Facebook Groups. All these groups are closed - only those bereaved parents in the groups can see the posts.

ONLINE FORUM
You can join the online forum by going on to the The Compassionate Friends website (www. tcf.org.uk). We ask you to complete a short form online (just so we know who is in the group to keep it safe for everyone) and you can then access The Forum to 'talk' with other bereaved parents. Posts are organised into topics so can be easily searched and conversations often continue for weeks or months.

Susan Hughes

SOME QUOTES FROM CURRENT FORUM USERS:
'After seven numbing months of family and friends saying all the wrong things, I needed to seek solace from people who 'got' me. Having a Forum to put down your thoughts is of great comfort, and whilst nothing can truly 'make it better',

experiencing the compassion of such caring lovely people who find the time to comfort others whilst dealing with their own grief, has gradually made this new life more bearable.'

Aly

'Living in the 'normal' world after the death of a child is immensely hard, How was it that many of these people, who I had known for most of my life, had not the slightest idea how crushed I was. I felt completely and utterly alone... until I found this amazing Forum. When I made contact, I was made to feel most welcome. It felt as if I had 'come home'. There were people out there just like me. Through their own shattering heartbreak they reached out to me offering unconditional love, warmth and care at a time when I wondered if I could go on.'

Linda

'The support I have received is truly amazing. There is no judgement. Only concern and genuine love. When we lose a child it can become so isolating, but the need to express our innermost feelings is so important. I feel this is my safe place. My lifeline. I have made so many friends here. I simply don't know how I would have survived without them.'

Deborah

'After my first post I received so many replies, some from people further down the line who were surviving and having happy times. It gave me hope. I was able to write down my darkest thoughts, and always someone would come back and say they'd had similar experiences. It was reassuring to know that other people also had days when they were too exhausted by grief to move. The Forum has truly been a lifeline and I don't know what I'd have done without it.'

Margaret

FACEBOOK GROUPS

We have a whole host of Facebook groups where bereaved parents and siblings can communicate - a bit like a 'virtual' support group. They are safe, secret groups, moderated by trained TCF volunteer bereaved parents/siblings. These groups offer support, encouragement, hope and friendship.

WE HAVE GROUPS FOR:

- *all bereaved parents*
- *parents with no surviving children*
- *parents bereaved by suicide*
- *parents bereaved by drug or alcohol use*
- *bereaved dads*
- *parents who have lost children to cancer or other long-term illness*
- *loss of a baby, toddler or preschool child*
- *brothers and sisters (over 18 years)*
- *Two Facebook groups (Compassionate Pals North and South) where bereaved parents can make arrangements for informal social meet ups.*

Some quotes from current members of the Facebook groups:
'I've been using TCF Facebook page for almost a year since my seven year old daughter died. My particular favourite elements are Photo Saturday (I deeply need to share my beautiful daughter with everyone) and Wednesday Wisdom - a very welcome chance to hear tiny snippets of positivity from people about what helps them get through this painful new life we all lead. Above all I am reminded that I'm not alone and that has been really helpful. It's like a new family where we stand shoulder to shoulder, honouring our wonderful children.'

Clare

'Here are the only ones that truly understand you. They are nonjudgmental and offer unconditional positive support. You

can draw strength from this group. They are always here so you are never alone.'

Gail

'I know that within the TCF Facebook group I will find a sympathetic ear and a shoulder to cry on. My online friends and I share the pain of losing a child and, as such, understand and feel for each other. Often within minutes of writing a post, I receive feedback - words of wisdom, wrapped up with encouragement and love. Sometimes a simple virtual hug or kiss is all I need to remind me that I'm not alone in my grief. TCF is truly all about friendship and support.'

Anne

'I am new to this group. I was feeling so sad and didn't know who to talk to about it. Reading about other people's experiences has helped me to realise my feelings are normal. It's good to be able to talk to others about thoughts and to be able to share photos without worrying about what people may think.'

Kirsten

'On the Facebook page I see the empathy shared between people. I see the sharing of memories and photos and experiences. I feel I can share things on that page without judgement and will always be supported. It's been a lifesaver for me.'

Sharon

Would you like to join an online group? If you'd like to take part in the Forum or the Facebook Groups, details of how to join can be found on the TCF website. www.tcf.org.uk Click on 'Find Support' then 'Online Support.'

***

On our facebook page 'Loss of a Child' we have a day where we try and write positive ideas. It's known as Wednesday

Wisdom. We all need a few wise pointers.

WEDNESDAY WISDOM
6th Feb 2019
by Bryan Clover

Let yourself enjoy things. If you are anything like me, there is a 'noise' in your head constantly, thoughts of our children whirling around in a 'white noise' that soaks up energy and capacity to think. It's exhausting. After Evie died I forgot to do the things I loved: cooking, baking and enjoying a decent glass of wine. I felt guilty if I enjoyed something because Evie wasn't there to share it.

But you know, I believe that we need to enjoy things if only for a short while. Just doing something for ourselves, something that we once loved gives our brains a respite from the pain, allowing it to heal and recover, and as importantly, rest.

It takes enormous energy and drive to force ourselves to sit and read, knit, cook something interesting or spend an hour on that hobby that once gave us pleasure. But we MUST do it. I'm now cooking again, and am teaching one of Evie's best friends to cook. Yes it's sad, but it's also productive. For a couple of hours each month, the noise in my head subsides a little and my blood pressure drops. Evie isn't there, but if I'm not fit and healthy then I can't work to preserve her memory.

If we look after ourselves, we can do more to make certain that our children's names are remembered by those around us.

SAY THEIR NAME

'They avoid speaking of your child to keep from upsetting you.They do not realise that no one ever speaking of them is your greatest fear.'

Do you speak of your child whenever you can? Do you say their name? I love to bring Nikki and Robin into the conversation but find it difficult with many old friends as they might not know what to say and you can imagine them thinking, 'I thought she'd got over that by now.' But when I'm with my TCF family I can say, 'Robin loved having a laugh. I bet he's with Jamie at the moment getting up to mischief.' And everyone smiles.

But being made to feel I shouldn't speak of my children makes me want to get up and leave the room…

The Elephant in the Room

*There's an **elephant** in the room.*
It is large and squatting, so it's hard to get around it.
Yet we squeeze by with, 'How are you?' and 'I'm fine'…
And a thousand other forms of trivial chatter.
We talk about the weather.
We talk about work.
*We talk about **everything else** - except the **elephant** in the room.*

*There's an **elephant** in the room.*
We all know it is there.
*We are thinking about the **elephant** as we walk together.*
It is constantly on our minds.
*For you see, it is a very big **elephant**.*
It has hurt us all.
*But we do not talk about the **elephant** in the room.*

Oh, please, say her name.
Oh, please, say 'Barbara' again.
*Oh, please, let's talk about the **elephant** in the room.*
For if we talk about her death, perhaps we can talk about her life?
Can I say 'Barbara' to you and not have you look away?
For if I cannot, then you are leaving me
Alone...
In a room...
*With an **elephant**.*

Terry Kettering, from 'Brothers and Sisters',
TCF Canterbury, Australia

SAY THEIR NAME

Say Their Name is a wonderful film made for TCF by Jane Harris and Jimmy Edmonds after their son, Josh, died in Vietnam in 2011. I have watched it several times - it's 16 minutes long - and is an inspired insight into what it is like for a parent who has lost a child or for someone who has lost their sibling. You can watch it on the home page of our TCF website at www.tcf.org.uk.

JANE - 'There was a remarkable feeling of closeness and a deepening and ongoing relationship with many of the interviewees. Regardless of the cause of our child or sibling's death, we'd all had very similar experiences. We'd all suffered a loss that was every parent's worst nightmare, we'd all had friends cross the road to avoid us, we'd all found ourselves stuck in some kind of time warp; and then there was the gob smacking realisation that every bereaved parent has at some moment had thoughts of ending their own life. But grief, I also learnt, is about love and just as there is no one way to love someone, so nobody can tell you how to grieve.'

JIMMY - 'We found much comfort from being able talk about Josh and the way we were feeling. Whatever crap emotions we have, whether it's the immense sense of loneliness, anger at other peoples' responses, guilt about not thinking about Josh enough, our fear of social occasions, the lack of confidence to be our true selves again; all these are somehow validated and made to feel OK by sharing them with other bereaved parents. It really helps to know that the ups and downs of our lives are perfectly normal - for us and for all bereaved parents.

'And that is really what the film is about - validating and normalising the experience of bereaved families trying to survive the death of a child. SAY THEIR NAME seems to work on all sorts of levels; it's good for the newly bereaved to know that there is hope beyond the horrendous darkness; it's good for professionals (counsellors, social workers, health workers, teachers) to have a better understanding of what it means to lose a child, and it's good for the non-bereaved who often feel at a loss themselves, unsure of how to support a friend or simply stuck in that 'don't know what to say' position.

'And it's been good for us too; we've been able to engage with and learn from others' experiences; we've been able to devote our emotional energy to a project that we really believe in. Above all it's kept us busy. Producing this video for TCF has given our lives new purpose.'

(You can find more of Jane and Jimmy's work on their website: www.thegoodgriefproject.co.uk)

CARRYING THE BURDEN

This Burden

I can not carry this burden alone
The road is too steep and the pain too great
I shall only get to the top of the hill
If I am able to lean on a firm shoulder whose strength
Lies in the reality of the feet which bear its weight.

The sharing of grief is the only solution
To the crisis that surrounds bereavement in our age.
To share a person's sorrow is to accept their reality
And to acknowledge the fact
That none of us is immune from death.

Simon Stephens, Founder of TCF

We often use the phrase 'weighed down by grief'. and the burden itself has been visualised in many concrete ways such as a stone, a heavy bag, or a trunk. Lynda Tomlinson has her own take on this.

MY COAT
by Lynda Tomlinson
In memory of my son, Gareth
Twenty four years ago my husband, Ben, dropped dead on the rugby pitch. Initially my grief felt like an enormous trunk that was chained to my ankle. At college, years earlier, I had a trunk just like that. It had travelled back and forth with me each year. It was silver with enormous padlocks and was my pride and joy. Now it had turned into a lead weight shackled to my ankle that I had to drag everywhere with me. It exhausted me and I hated it with a passion.

As the years passed the trunk morphed into a Gladstone bag. It had rather nice wooden handles. It was easier to manage but it was still heavy and really cumbersome.

Over the years the Gladstone bag morphed into a tapestry shoulder bag which I wore across my body. It nestled comfortably against my hip. In the bag were some sad memories but gradually more happy memories re-appeared and made their way into the bag. My bag had become somewhere where treasures lived. They comforted me when times were hard. The sadness had become softened by the precious memories.

As the years passed I experienced more losses, my mother, my aunts and uncles, friends and colleagues. Each became another shoulder bag which I treasured. Some were bigger than others but all contained sadness and treasures.

Then just before Christmas 2012 my 30 year old son lost his battle with alcohol. And back came the trunk tied to my ankle. Through my experience of loss I knew the trunk wasn't going to be with me forever and gradually Gareth's memories became a part of me to be treasured like all of the others.

By this time I was beginning to feel festooned with hippy shoulder bags. I loved the treasures they contained but they were starting to get a bit overwhelming. It was time for another 'morphing'. The shoulder bags became a beautiful coat with pockets where the memories and sadness nestle. Some pockets are big, others are small. The memories are all precious.

In May last year my older sister died after a short battle with cancer. Her pocket is new and rather raw but I know that gradually it will settle and become part of my coat.

The coat has many advantages. I can lay it down when I want to. I can huddle inside it when I need to but most of all I can keep my treasures near me and look at them any time I like.

There are times now when I can leave it somewhere safe and play and laugh again. Every year, a friend and I go to a sport and craft hotel. We 'put the world to rights' and play with paint and clay and glue. I leave my coat in my room but I know if I need it I can find it.

***

For Those who do not Understand

The grieving carry a heavy load.
You can add to it by judging,
criticising and forgetting

Or you can help,
Carry it for a while,
By listening, supporting
And remembering.

…Which will you choose?

Thanks to the unknown author

THE SNAIL
by Graham Foxley, Dad of Simon
For me, 'The Snail' represents the heavy burden that grief has imposed on my life, the isolation that I feel and the extent to which it has changed me.

I am not a poet - I have never (willingly!) read poetry nor attempted to write any - until our tragic loss. There is a state that I have discovered within myself, somewhere between deep sorrow and incapacitating depression, where my thought processes switch to poetry. The result has been over 50 poems in the past three years, a mathematician's poetry, short and to the point.

For me they have been a lifeline, enabling me to express emotions and grief that I could not achieve by talking.

The Snail

A snail heaves its shell across my window pane
It carries a heavy burden - I do the same
Its load grew with it - had time to adapt
Mine arrived without warning - no time to react
At first the weight crushed me - sat crying every day
Slowly I grew stronger - managed to crawl a little way

As the years passed I struggle to be
More like that person others wanted to see
They might not notice my slow heavy tread
Nor see my exhaustion or tiredness of breath
Unaware of the times the burden is too heavy again
When I curl up and hide from family and friends

I look for that snail - where can it be?
There was no snail - just a reflection of me....

Graham Foxley

Our children have died in many ways. Some have died suddenly through an accident, murder, suicide or unexpected illness. Others have died after a long illness or losing a battle with drugs. Whatever the cause of death, the burden of grief for us, bereaved parents, is exactly the same…

BUTTERFLY WINGS, BRICKS AND LEAD
by Tom Crouthamel, *TCF Sarasota FL USA*

When I saw HER load of grief, it looked to me to be merely a light load of butterfly wings as compared to my full load of heavy bricks. Then I saw another man and he seemed to be carrying a small load of lead. But as I watched her step on the scales bearing her load of butterfly wings, the scales read 'one ton'. When he stepped on the scales with his load of lead, the scales also read 'one ton'.

I knew my grief-load of bricks would weigh more, but those scales for me read 'one ton'. Our loads of butterfly wings, lead and bricks weighed exactly the same to the one who was carrying that particular load of grief.

We bereaved parents often feel resentment when a non-bereaved person speaks about our child's death. How can that person know or even dream of how I feel or what I am going through! These feelings may be justified. But when we begin to feel resentment towards another bereaved parent - 'That child's death was easy compared to my child's death.' 'I have suffered more than she/he ever did' - we should remember that each of our grief loads weighs two thousand pounds to the one under it.

Compared to Rose Kennedy, who had one child in a mental institution, and lost one daughter and three sons in violent deaths, my grief load begins to look as if it were made of gossamer soap bubbles, but when I again step on the scale, it still reads 'one ton'.

Our grief load may appear to weigh less because we who are under them have grown stronger through time and grief - process maturation. The load actually weighs no less; it is we who have grown stronger and can carry it more easily. Sometimes, we can even completely ignore the weight that is still there. Always be careful in judging another's grief load - remember that lead, those butterfly wings and those bricks, and how they all weigh the same to the one under that load of grief.

***

STEP BY STEP
I've carried this burden of grief twice and can reassure you that the weight you carry now WILL get lighter and the anger, disbelief, and all the other desperate thoughts and

emotions of early grief will begin to lift as you share your story with other bereaved parents and begin to recall the happy memories of your child.

Be patient with each other as we all find different ways through grief and we each take our own time as we tread this path. Don't beat yourself up when you find you're beginning to have moments when you laugh.

We can carry both grief and joy together as we learn how to move forward.

HOPE AND HEALING

Okay, so you're feeling as though you're going through a carwash on a bicycle, and all you can think of is, 'I hope this is going to end...'

HOPE... it's a four letter word for us; our child has died, what is there to hope for, to live for... We might have used the word everyday: 'I hope it's not going to rain' or 'I hope there's something left in the fridge so I won't have to go out shopping'. Now, all we can think of is, 'I hope this Pain will end...'

HOLD ON, PAIN ENDS
by Jane Killeen

My despair following my daughter's death from leukaemia was absolute. Hope grew very gradually and was only possible following changes I made in my thoughts and in the words I spoke, becoming more self-aware, realising my tendency to make it all about me and indulging in crippling self pity.

I was resisting life and the fact that life just is. Resistance promotes pain and despair; acceptance helped me to begin to see what had happened from a different perspective.

I put my daughter first, remembered her dignity and courage in coping with her illness and the treatment she undertook, and, ultimately, her acceptance of death. I believe I began to learn about real life once I had accepted that hope existed.

I began to believe that love was bigger than any circumstances or events. I started to look for examples of this and found them - sometimes in the big, public expressions of love and most often in small, everyday expressions of love that are easily missed in our complex and frantic world. I worked hard at this, as I did not want to return to the barrenness of despair.

Acceptance, surrender and love were my keys to hope - plus action and commitment to change from inside myself.

I learned to stop relying on outside stimulus to provide me with the things I thought I wanted to make my life enjoyable. Serenity is an inside job. Just a moment or two of it is worth waiting and working for. So, hold on, Pain ends.

***

Hope

It is the gift of Hope which reigns supreme in the attributes of The Compassionate Friends.
Hope that all is not lost.
Hope that life can still be worth living and meaningful
Hope that the pain of loss will become less acute
and, above all else,
the Hope that we do not walk alone,
that we are understood.
The gift of Hope
is the greatest gift that we can give those who mourn.
Simon Stephens, Founder of The Compassionate Friends

***

I felt hopeless at the start, utterly hopeless, and if you are very newly bereaved and feel like this too, I can say, truthfully, I know exactly how you feel.

It was meeting others further on in their grief journey that first gave me hope that it would not always be like this…

SOMEHOW IT'S SPRING
by Darcie Sims
Spring is the reawakening season… *the great wake up call for*

233

the earth. Somewhere, someone is answering that get up call... greeting the new season with vim, vigour, and vitality. There are smiles and renewed energy and hope seems to simply float on the softened air.

Somewhere... all of that is occurring, but not within me. It's still snowing inside my being. It's still winter inside here and there aren't any tulips about to burst open in my spirit. I've still got my snow boots on and the sun hasn't quite made it to my world. It's still winter inside me... I wonder if spring will ever come.

Oh, there have been moments of spring in the past. Wonderful, warm fleeting moments; moments when I 'forgot' about the pain, the emptiness, the despair, the grief. Moments when the world was right side up and the music made me dance. But they were only moments and I'm waiting for spring to arrive in me.

Hope... the major ingredient in spring, seems to elude my grasp. Just when I think there might be some hope, a memory comes creeping across my soul and it's winter again in my heart. It's this lack of hope that seems especially cruel during springtime. I thought this winter inside me would end and I was looking forward to a more peaceful time in my life. I thought we would settle down, plant a garden and live our life filled with memories and the opportunity to make new ones. HA! I thought grief would end at some point. The books all say it will... everyone else looks like their grief has subsided... how come spring missed us?!

A season without hope is the ultimate in despair and I've spent too many such seasons. Where does hope go and how do I get it back?

Hope is that elusive something that keeps us moving, even in the dark. We are only powerless when we have no hope, no vision, no faith in our own abilities. We may be helpless at times. We may question the arrival of spring but we are only truly powerless when we have no hope, no dreams…

Don't lose the hope! Search for it! Fight for it! Demand its return. Hope changes as we do and it can be so disguised that we may not recognise it, but it can be found - in the moments of our memories. We probably won't ever have totally happy lives again… We probably didn't have that kind of life anyway; we just thought we did.

Don't let death rob you of the moments of joy still to be remembered, and found. Don't let grief rob you of those spring places where love and joy live forever in the heart. Somewhere it is spring…

Deal with the anger, the guilt, the depression as it comes and then let it go as you can… so there is room for joy to come again. Let hope come in… it's spring.

***

Our Hope for You
This is our hope for you
    That the turmoil within you be stilled
And that you find calm
    That the anxiety within you be quietened
And that you find peace
    That the anguish within you be healed
And that you find joy
    That the gentle listening and understanding
Of those around you may help
    Your trust in life to be restored
Your faith strengthened
    And your hope return.
                Thanks to the unknown author

The bond between grieving parents is like no other. I shall never forget the welcoming words I heard when I first went to a residential weekend, 'Who are you here to remember?'. 'I'm remembering my daughter, Nikki', I said, and then years later it became, 'I'm remembering Nikki and Robin, who are you here to remember?'

In an atmosphere of calm and acceptance we were able to tell it exactly how it was, and in telling our stories we were saying, and admitting to ourselves, ever more deeply, 'I had a child who died'.

Over the months and years we will learn to say it more calmly. Each time we say it, we are learning our own terrible truth… our whole being will begin to shift in acknowledgement: I had a child who died.

And in acknowledging this, come healing.

FAITH, WONDER AND BEYOND...

In my book, *Don't Let Them Tell You How to Grieve* I wrote the following paragraph and poem:

I do not know what happens after death; my mind cannot grasp such an immense concept. I am content to wonder and let be what will be. I instinctively feel that all that great love which was in my children, that energy, cannot just have disappeared; it must be somewhere. When I die I will not have to leave them behind. They have gone through the barrier of death before me.

Facing Death
I do not fear death,
or even dying,
like some do.

For when it comes,
you will be waiting,
I will be with you.

We are all different. Some of us have a certainty of faith, whichever faith that may be, which supports and comforts us; some of us are still seeking. Some of us rail against a higher authority that has allowed the death of our loved one; some of us have made peace within ourselves which does not include any accepted religious beliefs. We work it out for ourselves. We are all different. And that's OK.

QUESTIONING
by Elly Hobbs
I had been a committed Christian for 45 years when our 29-year old son, Martin, who was a doctor, took his life.

I felt God had totally abandoned me and our family. All the promises in the Bible to those who love and serve the Lord were true, it seemed for every other family except mine. I could not read or sing Psalm 23.6, 'Surely goodness and mercy will follow me all the days of my life', without crying.

I never lost my faith and I was never angry with God, I just felt totally abandoned by the God whom I love. It was not until March 1996, when the Dunblane massacre took place, that paradoxically a little glimmer of light entered my darkness.

I was watching a service from the cathedral where the Rector spoke about the massacre and all the messages of sympathy he had received. One message made him very angry and he looked straight at me when he said that a lady had said to him, 'I do not understand the will of God,' and his reply was, 'This is not the will of God.' It was as if he was speaking directly to me about Martin's death.

Later in the service a man sang the 23rd Psalm and when he came to verse four, 'Yea though I walk through the valley of the shadow of death, I shall fear no evil… your rod and staff they comfort me', I thought, 'Yes, but I do not know how to lay hold of that rod and staff.'

I continued to exist somehow until March 1997 when I was in Israel and visited the Holocaust Museum, Yad Vashem, for the third time. I found myself crying with the Jews all the way through, identifying with them as they were stripped of everything, their clothes, their gold teeth, their jewellery, their dignity, and walked naked to the gas chambers.

They must have found it incomprehensible that their God, whom they had worshipped all their lives, would allow this to happen to them; and yet, they went singing to their deaths, knowing that they had no one else to put their trust in but God.

I felt that I too had been stripped naked before God, that He had taken away from me everything that I had built my faith on, and there was nothing left but Him. It was then I began to accept what had happened to my family, and gradually I have come to a place where peace and pain lie down together. But I will never be the person I was before my lovely son died. You do not go through such an experience without changing.

***

Remembering Kenneth Lawley
I spoke of you today... my son
At least of your death,
to friends
whose children have also died.
They understood
Thought of the plaque on the gates
of the Cemetery.
Alongside a similar one
in memory of the wife
of the founder of Rotary International
Simply said... 'this was
your last resting place',
here at Newington Cemetery, Edinburgh
and that your death
together with that of Billy Henderson
in May 1968 in Coventry, England
led to the founding of
The Compassionate Friends
the worldwide organisation
for the comfort and support of bereaved parents.
But is there where you lie?
Or have you spirited away
to another life
of which we have no comprehension?

Or do you stand with us, your loving family
as we change the flowers,
clean your headstone,
say a prayer
or make a promise?
I spoke of you today... my son
and I will be with you soon.
Joe Lawley

Written at a writing workshop during one of our TCF Weekends

***

I wonder if any of you have had a similar experience to the following:

A MOST PROFOUND EXPERIENCE
by Ruth Featherstone

John was only eight years old, my first-born son who was a loving, caring and very sensitive little boy. On 6th May 1996 he was on a day out with his dad and his younger brother, Darren, when he succumbed to a horrific accident. The emergency services were called and he was rushed to hospital by helicopter, where a team of surgeons tried for 3 hours to save his life. There, waiting in the corridor, I had the most profound experience of my life.

Suddenly I had this overwhelming sense of calm and complete peace. *I felt my body slump slightly to the left against a wall. My husband John thought I had fainted and went to seek help from a nurse. I knew I hadn't fainted and could hear everything that was going on around me.*

I felt my body enveloped with an overwhelming feeling of love and happiness, *and all my worries and concern about my son and what he was suffering at that moment in time left me.*

Even though my eyes were closed, I felt I could see a brightness radiating all around me. It felt like I was floating in an ocean of love.

The whole wonderful experience did not last more than a few minutes... Then a surgeon appeared at the door with the news no parent ever wants to hear, that my son had died from his injuries and they couldn't save him.

I always wish I could touch my loved ones and have them see and experience the love as I did that night, because the feeling is immeasurable and I can't explain the beauty and peace of it all. But I take from it the knowledge that I will definitely see my son again in heaven, which has given me the strength to cope every day with the pain of my loss.

I feel truly blessed that the passage of time has not dulled all that I felt and that everything I experienced that night is as vivid today as the day it happened, which has given my eternal spirit the strength I need to live my life the best I can for my family and everyone around me.

Before my experience happened I did believe in God but I never went to church or was a deeply religious person, but everything in my life changed from that moment. I know now God truly does exist...

BELIEVING THROUGH THE BAD BITS
by Audrie Norris

I certainly have no fear of death now as I know that Nick will be waiting for me. The temporary separation hurts a lot, more than anything I can imagine, but we have been given the strength to cope.

A lot of people asked how I could go on believing in God when something like that had happened, but my faith was the thing that kept me going most of all. I knew I couldn't have put my child into safer hands. To me, believing that everything is going right is the easy bit, but it doesn't mean anything unless I continue to believe through the bad bits as well.

***

I find the following speaks to me:

IN THE SPIRITUAL WORLD
by Peter Tatton-Brown
It was just five words on a quiet Sunday afternoon that changed our lives: 'Your son has been killed'. *An unbelievable shocking message. I was split into two parts, half knew what had to be done but the other half was paralysed.*

I should never see my son again, never hear him speak, never touch him and never tell him our news. Never, never, never - what a terrible word! Never again do what I so much loved. What a hellish thought. Never again tell him by a smile and a wink how much I loved him. Never, oh hateful word. My heart was cut out and I was overwhelmed by grief...

It is hard to find consolation in the written word, but it is there. Dear William Penn: 'And this is the comfort of the good, the grave cannot hold them...' We grasp at that hope and then, when quite unprepared, there is a feeling, a presence which cheers the heart. Yes, I am sure our son is still hereabouts...

Somehow in the depths I feel sure that life is continuous through the grave. *It is like a stitch of embroidery which appears above the canvas, runs along and is seen, then dips back below out of sight. The thread, the wool is continuous and only appears to disappear. Indeed I have a strong feeling that only humans need starts and finishes, beginnings and endings. In the real spiritual world there are no starts and ends, all space, time and life are boundless and eternal. This feeling is so* *strong it is now a great support.*

***

AND BEYOND...
by Iris Lawley MBE, parent co-founder of The Compassionate Friends

'Every day isn't a step away from Kenneth, it's a step closer to Kenneth.'

Kenneth died following a road accident where he was knocked off his bicycle on his way to school, leaving me in despair and crippled with grief. Every night he came to me in a dream with his head bandaged, saying, 'My head is sore, Mum.' I awoke distraught every morning and prayed for him to come to me and give a sign to let me know that he was now safe and happy.

After a very long and painful first year I had this dream - more than a dream, it was so vivid and clear. Kenneth was standing by the window in the hallway of our house in the school uniform in which we had him buried, he so loved his school. He no longer had bandages on his head and was just as he was in life, smiling his beautiful smile, and said, 'Look Mum, you don't have to worry about me anymore, I'm fine. You know, Mum, I don't have to go to school anymore.' I replied, 'Don't you son?' And he said, 'No, because now I know everything.' This has helped me through all these years without my beloved son.

The second visit came when I was rushed into hospital in an emergency following complications at the birth of my baby, Lisa, 22 months after Kenneth died. Lisa was drowning in the afterbirth and as they were sticking needles into me, I heard Kenneth say, 'Take my hand, Mum,' and I felt the pressure of his hand as he took mine. I know he saved us both, and Lisa, who never knew him in life, has a special closeness with him and she is his spitting image. These are the only two times in 32 years he has been back but on these occasions he saved both my sanity and my life.

CHOCOLATE

I was reading that great book 'Mindfulness' by Mark Williams and Danny Penman and came across the meditation on chocolate, so of course I had to try it. A good excuse to pop a bar of chocolate on my shopping list.

So, if you're ready, I'm going to try it out on you. Well, before we start, you need to go out and buy some chocolate. Choose one you've not tried before, or at least haven't eaten recently.

Ready? Right… Here we go:

- Open the packet and give a good sniff. Smell the chocolate, let it fill your nostrils.

- Break off a piece, no, don't put it in your mouth yet! Take a good look at it, examine it, let your eyes feast on it.

- Pop it in your mouth (that's the easy bit)

- Hold it on your tongue and let it melt (don't suck it)

- Concentrate on the chocolate. If you find your mind wandering, notice where it went, then gently bring it back to the present moment.

- When the chocolate has completely melted, swallow it very slowly and deliberately. Let it trickle deliciously down your throat.

- Do this all over again with the next piece.

How do you feel? Did the chocolate taste better than if you'd eaten it at your usual pace?

(Taken from **Mark Williams and Danny Penman's book**,

'Mindfulness, a Practical Guide to Finding Peace in a Frantic World.' Do read it; I found it a very useful book!)

Well, I tried it! I slipped a piece into my mouth while I was watching the Six Nations Rugby match between Wales and France on the television. I thought the Welsh had a good chance of beating the French even though they were playing away at the Stade de France. At half time the score was 16-0 to France. Extremely frustrated and disappointed, I slipped a piece of chocolate into my mouth and began to meditate…

I'm sure this wasn't supposed to happen: I fell asleep and woke to see the last few minutes of the match with Wales winning 24 -19, and my mouth full of the most delicious melted chocolate you could imagine! (I have since watched the second half - and I've finished the chocolate!)

BEFORE WE GO ON TO MORE CHOCOLATE I'd like to share with you this short piece on Meditation on Grief.

MEDITATION ON GRIEF
by Jack Cornfield

To meditate on grief, let yourself sit, alone or with a comforting friend. Take the time to create an atmosphere of support. When you are ready, begin by sensing your breath. Feel your breathing in the area of your chest. This can help you become present to what is within you. Take one hand and hold it gently on your heart as if you were holding a vulnerable human being. You are.

As you continue to breathe, bring to mind the loss or pain you are grieving. Let the story, the images, the feelings comes naturally. Hold them gently. Take your time. Let the feelings come layer by layer, a little at a time.

Keep breathing softly, compassionately. Let whatever feelings are there, pain and tears, anger and love, fear and sorrow, come as they will. Touch them gently. Let them unravel out of your body and mind. Make space for any images that arise. Allow the whole story. Breathe and hold it all with tenderness and compassion. Kindness for it all, for you and for others.

***

'When after heavy rain the storm clouds disperse,
is it not that they've wept themselves clear to the
end?'
Ghalib

***

Right, now for more chocolate…

THERE'S NO COMFORT IN A CARROT
by Darcie Sims
I know… I know… I shouldn't seek comfort from the refrigerator. Food is not the solution, but, at times, it does seem to ease the pain. Maybe it simply masks the moment, but it also gives me something to do later as I sweat off those extra calories. I know about food and nutrition and self-esteem, and I know, too, that comfort does not come in bottles, boxes or bags of chips. I know that food is only a temporary source of solace that will turn into a long-term battle of the bulge. But there are some days when all that knowledge simply leaves me aching and wishing for some chocolate.

*I've been on this journey through grief more than once and I've learned a lot about coping skills, healthy choices and positive affirmations. I've also learned that sometimes what I really want is chocolate. There's no comfort in a carrot, but when there are no words left to say, **when the pain is overwhelming and the helplessness sweeps over us, there is always chocolate!***

Some days are worse than others. Some are not worth

remembering and some should not have been allowed to happen. I don't know who is in charge of those days, but I would very much like to speak to that person. Some days are just not worth having. They move so slowly that even the sun gets bored and simply falls from the sky in a rush of despair. Some days the sun is smarter than I am, and it just doesn't get up. Some days are rain-filled while others are shrouded in gloom. Some days are painful, while others just seem empty.

Oh, there are some good days, too. In fact, there are some pretty wonderful days, but we don't seem to remember them as well as we recall the awful ones. Somehow, the tough days get relived more often in our memory and the hours of darkness seem longer than the hours of light.

Some days I need chocolate. *If I am lucky enough to suffer only from an occasional 'down' day, then my usual coping techniques of sleeping late, eating a real egg and watching a good movie (while consuming semi-indecent amounts of popcorn) generally suffice. I've read enough and lived long enough to realise that those days will eventually pass, especially if I do not ignore them. And so, I have learned to cope with those days that simply should not have happened.*

But, once in a while, once in a great while, one of those days turns into one of those weeks and maybe even into one of THOSE MONTHS, and suddenly I can't remember anything decent, lovely, worthwhile or fun. It is as if my memory banks have been erased of all joy, and the sun only casts shadows of sorrow. Those days, when we can't remember his smell, the sound of her voice or the touch of his hand, are the days we fear the most.

Those days, when pain sweeps over us like searing flames, are the days we lose even the light, and then hope seems an

empty place. Those are the days that are meant for chocolate.

On those days, we may discover we need more than a good book, a bowl full of popcorn and a box of tissues. On those days, what we need is comfort, companionship, courage... and chocolate. Surviving an attack of those days can test the wit and wisdom of even the best of us. All the tricks of the trade just don't seem to touch the emptiness, and that's when we have to call in the reinforcements.

On those days, there is no comfort in a carrot. But, oh, the caring compassion of a friend bearing chocolate! *I'm not sure if it is the chocolate or the friend that lifts the gloom, but I do know the silent blessing of a phone call from a concerned and loving friend, the gentle touch of a companion and best of all, the shared joy of a warm, chocolate-chip cookie.*

Without a friend, those days are glum indeed. Friends know when to talk and when to listen. They know they cannot erase the guilt we carry or talk us out of our despair. They do not try to cheer us up, but neither do they drag us down. They know when to call, when to come and when just to stand silently close... trusting. They offer prayers, poems and pastries. A friend will go jogging FOR us (HA!) and always says how nice our hair looks!

The gift of friendship goes beyond the mere exchange of gifts and into the magical space created by love. A friend doesn't have to bring food - doesn't even have to come! **We can simply feel a friend's caring, even when it comes from thousands of miles away. We are connected through compassion, caring, cookies, carrots and chocolate... (CARROTS?!)**

A friend helps us remember and helps us to heal. *So make this day a National Friend's Day and send a card, a cookie, a casserole or a carrot (it could be a chocolate carrot) to say,*

'Thanks for being my friend! Thanks for caring, for calling, for cooking, for cleaning, for coming. Thanks for being a part of my circle... for being a part of me. Thanks for helping me skip the cookie and embrace the moment. Thanks for jogging with me, for believing in me and for loving me. Thanks for not sending chocolate but visualising it instead!'

Thanks for YOU, my friends. Someday there will be a fat-free chocolate! But by then, I won't need it anymore because I have finally learned it is the gift of YOU that gives the greatest comfort! There's no comfort in a carrot, but oh, the magic of YOU sharing it with me!

SYMBOLS

I'm waiting, but there's no sign yet…

It's morning again and I'm sitting at my patio window with my first cup of tea… The rains of yesterday have gone and the lower part of the garden where the old apple tree stands is streaked with sunshine.

I'm trying out a ground bird feeder. It has a tray and a cage you can put over it to stop larger birds and squirrels getting in. A blackbird has come to investigate. He has no problem with the cage; he hops in and immediately goes to work on the buggy nibbles, then flies away. Buggy nibbles are a mix of mealworms, suet and cereal and the birds love them. I look again; there is another blackbird. Is it the same blackbird who comes, I wonder, or a different one?

I'm waiting, but still no sign …

The little wren has come. It's lovely to see her because she's a very rare visitor. She never goes near the cage but scuttles along the fence in the periwinkle and aubretia, presumably picking up insects. She's come for her grub you could say…

….. And, at last, there's the robin. He's come. He stands on the lawn looking at me. My heart lifts. It takes me back to the time just after Robin died when I was in Wales and parked near a bay on the Gower coast. It was pouring with rain and I was feeling desolate. A robin flew down and perched on a branch of the hedge just in front of the bonnet of my car. I held my breath but there he stayed, not leaving me. We sat together for some time… I decided to start the car and go before he could fly off and leave me…

A WHITE FEATHER

My lovely friend, Maria, says that her son, Jamie, has a way of making his presence felt. Whenever a white feather floats down she knows that Jamie is near.

One morning I came down and noticed a white feather sticking up in between the paving stones on my patio. Right beside it was a robin… I stood very still, watching the robin and white feather together. Later I emailed Maria, 'Jamie and Robin have got together. Watch out for mischief.'

FEATHERS
by Maria Ahern

I remember vividly the first time that feathers came into my life. I was in the garden with my niece. James had been gone just a few days. My niece spotted it. A beautiful, perfect white feather on my shoulder. Such a contrast from the black clothes that I was wearing.

'Look', she exclaimed… 'Feathers appear when angels are near'. I'd never heard this phrase before but I was comforted by the notion. Now, as I see feathers drop in front of me I say, 'Hello son', and maybe I will blow him a little kiss.

The killjoys remind me that feathers just come from birds who fly in the sky. Of course that is correct and I don't for one minute imagine that James carries a basket of feathers and sprinkles them for me to see. That just isn't James' style. However, I can't explain how they appear in the oddest of places. How is it that a feather can land right at my feet with no bird in sight? How does it cling to my windscreen in the rain as I get into my car, just long enough for me to see? How do they appear in my handbag or in my living room just when I need them to?

I don't know the answers to these questions but I do know that every time I see one, I smile and say, 'Hello son' and being able to say these words, even to a feather, is indeed a gift. So logic and fact can go out of the window as far as I'm concerned. In my book, 'Feathers appear when angels are near'.

***

BUTTERFLIES

Butterflies are seen by some people as deep and powerful representations of life. Around the world people view the butterfly as representing endurance, change, hope and life.

I'm sure I'm not the only one who has happened upon a butterfly and is captivated by its beauty and ethereal quality. Some people have a very personal experience of a butterfly:

CHRISTMAS BUTTERFLY
by Audrie Norris

Christmas morning 1997, and we were sitting in the quaint little village church next door but one to our cottage, when I and others around us, by the sound of hushed whispers, were aware of a butterfly happily flying around amongst the worshippers.

After a few minutes flying around and inspecting various people, this beautiful creature came to rest on the deep stone recessed windowsill next to me and gently folded its wings. The service had not long started, and it remained there throughout. At one stage I ventured to touch its wings very gently with a kiss from my fingertips, mentally saying, 'Happy Christmas', to it. I was frightened this might make it fly away but no, it stayed.

At the end of the service I was more bold with it and, although I felt I did not want to go away and leave it, John knew what was in my heart and reminded me that I must let go. Reluctantly I planted an even stronger kiss on its little wings, wishing it goodbye and thanking it for being with us. It sat still, but as I reached the church door I looked back and it had flown away. While the rest of the villagers were remarking on the unusual sight of a butterfly in church on Christmas Day, I knew it was more than a butterfly. My cynical elder son would say, 'pure coincidence, mother', but I know it was Nicolas.

***

'A butterfly lights beside us, like a sunbeam
and for a brief moment its glory and beauty
belong to our world - but then it flies on again,
and although we wish it could have stayed
we are so thankful to have seen it at all.'

***

I am in the Light

When you see a butterfly, dancing colours flying by
A willowy feather rising high, and a gentle pink rose,
  soft as a sigh
When a colourful rainbow appears in the sky
You will know, I am standing by

I am still sparkling, I am nearby
The shiniest star you can see in the sky

Like the joy I brought you while I was here
I am glistening inside every tear
I am shining, I am bright, I am Lauren, I am in the light
I am the butterfly, the rainbow and the rose
I am that feather but in different clothes

I am always beside you, each step that you take
I sit and think with you, each decision you make
I walk with you, talk with you and feel you so near
Although you can't see me, I hold you so dear

I am always with you and will always be there
Every breath that you take, I am in the air
Think of me singing a song so sweet
In a beautiful place where one day we will meet
Till then I am sleeping in heavenly peace

It hurts me, your pain, but please understand, I'm safe
* and happy*
I'm holding your hand

I am always with you.

Bridget Eley

***

The Butterfly Story

I heard Margaret Marsh share her reflections on the life cycle of the butterfly over 20 years ago when we were both part of a TCF Group in Carshalton, Surrey. Since then I have shared this butterfly story at a residential weekend and read it at our candle lighting ceremony in Colchester. However tempted we are to 'make people better' we need patience to wait until a person is ready to leave their 'chrysalis'.

Maureen Lahiff

THE LIFE CYCLE OF THE BUTTERFLY
by Margaret Marsh

The image of the butterfly emerging from the chrysalis is very meaningful for those whose loved ones have died. It certainly spoke powerfully to me after the death of my son, about my hope that new life comes from the darkness of death, just as the butterfly emerges from the chrysalis. Indeed, I am always comforted by the thought whenever I see a butterfly.

It came as a gentle reminder especially during a Quiet Day I attended some time later when we were invited to reflect on the life cycle of the butterfly. Of course my initial thought was for my son, but I suddenly found myself pondering on my own grief journey - the way life had been so unexpectedly changed and how I had been plunged into a grief so intense that I had never experienced before.

It occurred to me how often we are like contented little caterpillars, happily munching our way through life, our horizon limited to the edge of our own particular cabbage leaf. And then, often without warning, we are plunged into a very dark place - like a chrysalis - and everything changes. The comparisons of being in the chrysalis and the experience of grief is remarkable.

Just like the butterfly, we are in the dark. It's a very lonely place; there is no apparent way forward, no way back, and no way out. What we are not aware of is the enormous changes that are taking place within the chrysalis. The butterfly begins to form and grow and change. And so we, in our grief, do not remain static. We too are re-formed by the experience - and it takes time.

How long we remain there will vary for each one, as the way we experience grief is utterly unique for all of us. All we know is that the longer we are there the more uncomfortable it gets.

And just when it seems that all is lost, suddenly a chink of light appears and as the butterfly instinctively moves towards the light, so do we. Gradually the light gets bigger as the chrysalis begins to split. The butterfly emerges, takes its wings and flies. How different life looks now. It will never be a caterpillar again. And we, too, are able to break out into a new place, to see life from a different perspective, to have a different understanding. We shall never be the same person again.

For those who seek to walk with us through our grief, there is an important lesson to learn. There is always the temptation to 'make it better' for it is not easy accompanying another who is grieving. But the chrysalis phase cannot be rushed. Indeed, if anyone tried to release the butterfly before it was ready it could result in damaging it or, at worst, killing it. So we need friends who will accept us just where we are, supporting us every step of the way, and waiting with love for the time when there is an emergence into new life. It will come, as I discovered myself.

The scars of grief remain, but they are no longer open wounds. And so we become 'wounded healers' for others, able to accompany them through the journey of grief with an understanding that comes from experience.

***

Looking out into the garden again:
There's a baby sparrow on the fence, its little beak open. Its dad has fed it three times…

Mr Blackbird is on the patio. He's dropped a buggy nibble, possibly it's a bit large for him to tackle all at once. A sparrow has just nipped in and nicked it. But another sparrow has come too and is trying to grab it from the other one's beak. It's broken, and now they have half each.

I wonder if Robin will come again…

THE ORCA WHALE
by Elly Sutherland
I've been following this story about the orca whale carrying her dead calf in a grieving ritual. The other whales in her pod have been helping her along but she is falling behind them, at last report, as they go on their journey. There is such a spiritual parallel between these gentle creatures and our human grief especially when it involves the death of our child.

I would have physically carried my children with me if it were possible. I told the funeral director when Rachel died that I wanted to keep her at the funeral home so I could sit by her any time and for as long as I wanted. Sadly, I was unable to see my James due to the circumstances and that is a decision I will always ponder. I do carry them metaphorically, pushing them along with me and, like the whale momma, I have to periodically let go of them to tend to the business of life, always picking them up again to continue my journey. I will never let go.

The whale momma has lots of support to carry her dead calf as the other pod members surround her in a ritualistic dance. However, it is reported that she is falling behind as they push ahead for their own survival.

And there you have it. As time passes I've found myself falling behind the pod as it were. It's not that the love and support isn't still there but more a case of people going on with their lives. This is not some kind of malicious neglect. It's perfectly normal. I fall behind because there are no engagements, graduations, weddings, grandchildren, recovery celebrations, birthdays and such, so I swim at the back of my pod carrying my lifeless, beautiful children as I try to stay engaged with the rest of the world. It is true to say I do have company back there with other friends who are swimming beside me carrying their children. We nudge each other along constantly and have a ritualistic dance of our own quite separate from the normal expected life dance.

Sometimes I cry out with the pain from the weight I carry, not wanting to let go for one second. It is overwhelmingly tiring and treading water is all I can manage. Quite often someone in my pod drops back, giving me a huge push to help me along. They do this by acknowledging my memories, speaking the names of my children or sharing stories and photographs.

The whale momma has quite different priorities in her life yet we are one and the same. There is always someone in your pod who needs help to keep swimming for many reasons. Don't let them fall behind. Do that ritualistic dance around them and make sure they are not lost to the deep dark lonely waters with no help in sight. Reach out your hand and hold theirs for a while to keep them swimming. Or even a fin if that applies…

***

And in the garden…

ASHLEY WAKELIN, THE LEGEND
From a bereaved Dad
Dear Ash

Nearly two decades ago I picked an acorn. It was perfectly formed, shiny, full and young. I helped nurture the acorn. I loved it, watered it and fed the acorn.

Sometimes the acorn needed more, and it got more. The acorn grew. Its roots grew. The roots became strong and touched other roots of other trees that began to grow around it. The roots became entwined with others, so entwined that the roots would never be able to be separated from those they touched.

The acorn grew and grew. I encouraged it to find water and food for itself. I let it grow. It reached up into the sky. High. Strong. It was majestic. The acorn had grown into a mighty oak tree, now much bigger than me. We sheltered under its branches from the rain. We used its shade when it was hot. The oak tree protected us all. We rested in its thick branches. We enjoyed being around that oak tree. It was special. Occasionally we walked by the oak tree without looking; yet the branches would reach out in the wind, wrap around us and pull us to its trunk.

Then the worst day ever. It only happens in films doesn't it? 'I'm sorry to have to tell you...' was what the police officer said. He asked me to go and see the oak tree. It had been felled. Yes, it was our oak tree. It was the tree that had grown from an acorn so long ago. I looked at the oak tree through my tears. The acorn had grown into such a beautiful oak tree. It was so beautiful, strong and young that inside me screamed to know why?

The oak tree's roots remain. They are still wrapped round us all. They grew towards our roots for a purpose, to be close to us. I look at the oak tree now where it was placed, against the skyline, reaching higher to the sky and wider to us all. You might think that the oak tree isn't there anymore. Well you are wrong. I can still see it. I feel its roots. I see it still there. Strong, reaching up, and I know if I need protection it will offer it to me. I don't even need to ask. It's evergreen.

Forever and ever we will be, forever you and me. I love you Ash,

Dad

***

This following piece by Sue Fern touched me deeply. No matter how long or hard we tried, our daughter, Nikki, could not, in the end, respond to the love and care which we gave her.

ON A ROSEBUSH FULL OF BLOOMS
by Sue Fern
In loving memory of Dominic Archer-Fern who died on 3/3/10 aged 14. He was, to me, a delicate rosebud that never reached his full potential but was beautiful nonetheless.

On a rosebush full of blooms, there is occasionally one rose more fragile than the rest. Nobody knows why. The rose receives the same amount of rain and sun as its neighbouring blooms; it receives the same amount of water and food from the earth, of clipping and tending and gentle encouragement from the gardener. Its time on earth is neither more nor less signifiant than that of other blooms alongside. Its stresses are neither greater nor fewer. Its promises of development are just as rich. It has all the necessary components to become what it is intended to be: a beautiful flower, fully open, spreading its petals, fragrance and colour for all to see.

Once in a while a single rose doesn't reach maturity. It's not the gardener's fault. It's not the fault of the rose. For some roses, even the touch of the gentle spring rain leaves bruises on the petals. The sun's rays - so soft and warm to some flowers - feel searing to others. Some roses thrive while fragile ones feel buffeted by inner and outer ghost-winds.

So it is that sometimes, despite the best growing conditions, the best efforts of the gardener, and the best possibilities and predictions for a glorious blooming season, a particularly fragile rose will share its glow for a while, then fade and die. And the gardener and the rosebush and the earth and all around grieve.

We are never ready for a loss, not for the loss of a promising rosebud, nor for the loss of a friend or relative whose life appears ready to uphold with brilliant colour and fulfilment. In the midst of our grieving, we can remember and celebrate the glimpses of colour, fragrance and growth that were shared. We can love the fragile rose and the fragile soul for the valiant battles won and the blooming that was done. And as our own petals unfold, we can remember the softness and beauty of those who touched us along the way.

REMEMBERING

*'Don't try to destroy a beautiful part of your life
because remembering it hurts.
As children of today and tomorrow,
we are also children of yesterday.
The past still travels with us and what it has been
makes us what we are.'*
Earl A Grollman

WALK TO REMEMBER

On the Sunday morning at our National Gathering weekend, two of our members, Pat and Jerry Morris, have for many years organised a walk to remember our children, grandchildren and siblings. We walk round the beautiful grounds of the hotel and end up at a willow tree where we tie ribbons for each of our children on the branches. It is a very beautiful and comforting way to honour our children. We stand around the tree and read poems, including the following:

We Remember Them
*At the rising of the sun and its going down
we remember them*

*At the blowing of the wind and in the chill of winter
we remember them*

*At the opening of the buds and in the rebirth of spring
we remember them*

*At the blueness of the skies and in the warmth of summer
we remember them*

*At the rustling of the leaves and in the beauty of autumn
we remember them*

At the beginning of the year and when it ends
we remember them

As long as we live, they too will live;
for they are part of us, as we remember them

When we are weary and in need of strength
we remember them

When we are lost and sick at heart,
we remember them

When we have joy we crave to share,
we remember them

When we have decisions that are difficult to make,
we remember them

When we have achievements that are based on theirs,
we remember them

As long as we live, they too, will live;
for they are now a part of us, as we remember them.
Sylvan Kamens and Rabbi Jack Riemer

***

Memories
When you need to…
reach deep inside and take out one of your precious
memories,
wipe away the cobwebs, lay it out in front of you,
and let the sunshine and the sounds engulf you.
Revel in the experience of it…
relive each precious moment, be overwhelmed by them
and taste the wonderful sweet tears that are their gift.
When your needs have been almost satisfied
pause for one more second

then gently fold it back up, give it a big hug and tender kiss,
and return the treasure to where you found it…
Then to make the experience complete,
find someone special and share the feelings with them,
for surely this is something meant to be shared!
Don't be afraid of using them - that's what memories are for,
you will never lose them… for as certain as the sun will rise
tomorrow,
love, once attained, is never lost.
Steve Channing

COPING WITH MEMORIES
by Jenny Kander, TCF Johannesburg, S A

Memories are a bridge between the past and the present. In an abstract, though nonetheless real sense, you can reach your child, be with him or her, by crossing the bridge (remembering); but herein lies the pain - you have to go back to the past because he or she is not physically present.

The memories that you have of your child, whether of happy or unhappy times, or perhaps of how he or she looked, felt, sounded, all these are precious, special and sometimes can be so painful that you want to block them to escape the anguish. This is normal, natural. We would all like to escape from pain. And yet the loss of your memories would leave a huge gap.

Perhaps the most difficult to deal with are the sudden, unexpected stabs that can occur anytime. When an association with your child comes out of the blue - perhaps a piece of music or a can of spaghetti in the supermarket - whatever it is that throws you, try to remember to breathe deeply and slowly, and it will help. **Remembering is important because even when it is painful, healing is taking place.**

Mother's Day - *From a mother to her child Michael, I wrote this poem for you x*

*My child, how I remember holding your tiny little hand
when you were little,
The way your fingers grasped mine.
The way your hair curled at your neck.
The way it tickled my face when you slept on my shoulder.
My child, how I remember how you hid behind my legs
when you were shy,
The way your eyes looked around to see if it was safe
and the way your eyes scanned a room,
checking I was still there.
I close my eyes and still smell your child like aroma
and the chubbiness or your little body next to mine.
My child, how I remember you growing up
and the way we used to measure your height on the wall.
The day your feet were bigger than mine
and you looked over my shoulder
when we looked in the mirror.
Yes I remember when you said that you loved me
and you would be alright and not to worry
as you were all grown up!
Yes I remember.
I will always remember, as you are my child
and those memories are mine alone as your mother.
Precious and tucked away in my thoughts,
bringing smiles and sadness.
So as time passes, I will never forget
and I will always be your mother
and you will always be my child.*

Sue Brooks

Memories
will bring you love from the past
Courage in the present
Hope for the future
Sascha Wagner

Sometimes

Sometimes,
Memories are like the rain showers
Sprinkling down upon you
Catching you unaware.

Sometimes,
Memories are like thunderstorms
Beating down upon you,
Relentless in their downpour
And then they will cease,
Leaving you tired and bruised.

Sometimes,
Memories are like shadows
Sneaking up behind you
Following you around,
Then they disappear
Leaving you sad and confused.

Sometimes
Memories are like comforters
Surrounding you with warmth,
Luxuriously abundant,
And sometimes they stay,
Wrapping you in contentment.
Thank you to the unknown author

How many of us, from time to time, take out something our child used to wear, hold it close to us, the feel and smell of it bringing back memories of our child. I wear a dressing gown that used to belong to Nikki and when I'm gardening in the summer I wear a shirt of Robin's. What should we do with our child's clothes? I'm sure you've wondered that at one time or another.

Perhaps we've passed some of them on to other members of the family or to a charity but there are usually some particular clothes we can't bear to part with tucked away in the wardrobe or hanging on a peg…

Metamorphosis

On impulse I take her almost new, blue
Rain jacket from the peg behind my own -
Untouched for two years or more
Since last worn by its owner who is gone.
I zip it on, and imperceptibly
My own shape changes to hers,
Uncannily - since we were not the same.
The jacket's tailoring masks my extra girth
So I appear neat and trim as she was,
Ready for action, adventures unknown.
Her navy boy's cap completes the image
Of one many years younger than I;
The athletic, androgynous figure
Beneath whose lean exterior lies
The eternal female, warm and wise.
Somewhere in another realm
Her essence lives on in undiluted spirit,
Travelling through that unknown kingdom
Of the soul, in realms so bright -
While we, earthbound, recall her as she was
In the fading, soft autumn sunlight.

Carol Wain

THE BENCH
by Pat Morris

Our church runs a luncheon club for stroke patients every Thursday and my friend, Liz, and I are volunteers. Every other year we take our members away on holiday. This year we took them to Weston-Super-Mare.

On our last day, Liz, also a bereaved parent, and I managed an hour to ourselves in a little cove near our hotel. On our way back to the hotel we found a lovely bench with a plaque on. We read the following:

> **For Bereaved Parents and their families**
> **A place to sit, reflect and find comfort**
> **'To live in hearts we leave behind is not to die'**
>
> *Donated by a mother in memory of her son,*
> *Jaques Burton-Lawl 23.4.94 to 27.08.06*

So we sat, reflected, and found comfort.

***

I do not ask
that you forget your dear departed.
I want you to remember.
I only ask that you remember
more than the moment of death,
more than the funeral,
more than the house of mourning.
Remember Life!
Remember the whole Life.
Not the final page of it.
Rabbi Maurice Davis

ACCEPTANCE - OR NOT

'Whatever you can accept will bring you peace.'

I had great trouble in accepting this concept. I would never be able to accept the death of my daughter - and then my son. It was impossible. Then I read another similar, slightly longer, quotation:

*'Whatever you can accept will bring you peace,
including that you are in resistance, that you
cannot accept.'*

I had to think hard about that one. It means, I think, that if you **accept the fact** that you will **never be able to accept** the death of your child, that too will bring you peace.

That brought me up short. So the important thing was to **accept** that I could **never accept** the fact that my daughter and son had died. And accepting that fact would bring me peace. I expect you're thinking about that too!

THOUGHTS ON GRIEF AND ACCEPTANCE
by Margaret Hayworth
One of the basic human emotions that cannot be denied is love. So that when a loved one dies, grief is the result. Death may happen quickly but to work through grief takes time.

Grief presents a myriad of feelings. These vary in duration and intensity according to social conditions and the mode of death. Some who have studied the effects of bereavement identify stages of grief. Whatever terms are used, 'acceptance' is always the final one.

Acceptance is defined by Elisabeth Kubler Ross as **'a feeling of victory, a feeling of peace, of serenity, of positive submission** *to things we cannot change'.*

Acceptance can occur with the abatement of normal grief reactions but this is not always so. For acceptance to occur, ways and means have to be found to handle normal grief reactions and at the same time a philosophy of life is needed.

Some already possess a faith which carries them through unquestioningly. Others find their beliefs are challenged. For many in this secular, scientific era a philosophy is not something that has been actively sought. Death presents us with man's - and woman's - mortality and hence questions such as 'Why?', 'What is life and death all about?', 'Is there immortality?', 'What form does it take?', 'If death is felt to be final, what sense can be made of the lives of our departed ones?'.

To come through the grief process to an acceptance *it seems necessary to spend half of one's time actually thinking and talking about one's child and one's reactions. Also to search for a philosophy of life that feels comfortable to oneself. The other half of our lives needs to be taken up by work and other pursuits. Many find doing something for others very beneficial.*

Many feel that each individual mind is incapable of perceiving the whole. What it does see and feel is part of the Ultimate Reality, God, Supreme Being, Universal Mind, or whatever term one wishes to use. Each person's path to his/her understanding will be his/her own individual experience. This can come via any religion or none. **What is important is to know why we feel as we do.**

This I firmly believe is the path to acceptance; and to Elisabeth Kubler Ross's definition, I would add joy and a much more meaningful life. I shall always be grateful for my daughter's life and death. She has taught me so much. I continue to love her dearly and, yes, I do miss her physical presence very much.

WHAT ACCEPTANCE IS ABOUT
*by **Dennis Klass**, TCF South Africa*

There is an interesting discussion in the Talmud, an ancient Jewish writing. Those Jews had the custom of rending their garments - literally tearing their clothes - to symbolise the ripping apart that death brings. But the question was raised, after the period of mourning, could you sew the garment up and use it again?

The teachers answered yes, but when you mended it, you should not tuck the edges under so it would look as if it had never been torn. This symbolised the fact that life after grief is not the same as before. The rent will show. The next question was, can you sell that garment? The teachers answered no. The rending and ending of our life is ours and others cannot wear it.

*That is what acceptance is about. It is possible for the family to learn to say, '**What has happened has happened.'***

We cannot fully understand why, or why it happened in our family. We would not wish the experience on anyone else, for it has been very hard. We cannot just pick up the threads of life and pretend nothing has happened - our garments are rent. But through that experience perhaps we can say we are more sensitive to the needs of others, perhaps have a bit more love and compassion. Not only do we NOT want to sell our rent garments, we want to wear them as a sign of hope for others.'

People need to absorb that death experience into their own Horizons of Understanding, into their own Meaning Systems. Then they can accept healing, look death in the eye and say, 'You are neither good nor bad, you are merely part of the common human lot'.

***

As the years go by we learn to live with our grief - but acceptance is something else. I didn't accept all at once, of course I couldn't. But after the first utter disbelief and years of acute grief when all I could think of was wanting my children back, I came to accept bit by bit. I began to:

Accept that my daughter and son had died - that took a long time to sink in. They say it's a long distance between the head and the heart.

Accept that the pain of my grief would last a long time and I just had to work through it.

Accept that although the pain was easing, I would always miss them; there would be a huge hole in my life.

Accept that I couldn't change the past and I had to try to live a worthwhile life in the name of my two children.

And now, a feeling of peace and serenity that despite everything, and accepting I can never have my children back physically, but keeping them present in my heart always, things are as well as they can be.

It has taken me a long time to come to what might be termed 'acceptance'. I have worked through my grief over the years, but it has been a long journey. If you are newly bereaved or even a few years down the line and know in your heart that you will never be able to accept the death of your child, then that's okay. Just try and remember the saying:

> **'Whatever you can accept will bring you peace, including that you are in resistance, that you cannot accept.'**

THE POEM BELOW was written by a young man, Harry Corder Greaves, who used to come to our Quaker meeting. He was a gifted craftsman and made a bookcase for our foyer and carved a beautiful design on it.

He went missing a couple of years ago; his body was eventually found in a ravine in the mountains near Pisac, Peru, where he had gone solo trekking. Harry had an adventurous spirit and knew what he wanted to do - and did it. He wrote this poem just before he set out...

Faith

Faith is opening the door
and allowing the universe to step through
We all have wounds
a change of perspective makes them gifts

We all have a path to tread
Accept it joyfully
It is your blessing and your teacher
Trust is accepting life is beyond my control

Let life carve me
as the river carves the mountains
Give me deep valleys of experience
And the high peaks of expanded awareness

Let me walk this trail with eyes wide open
With the sun and the wind
and the rain upon my face
Let me taste life and when I die
Let me know that I have lived

Harry Corder Greaves

CHANGING AND GROWING

*'I can be changed by what happens to me, but I
refuse to be reduced by it.'*
Maya Angelou

When I think back over the years I remember how I used to react when someone said to me,'You'll get over it'. I felt utter disbelief followed by fury. How dare they? I hadn't had a bout of flu; my child had died. My world as I knew it had ended; how could I ever get over the death of my child?

I suppose they thought, 'she was leading a normal happy life before this happened, give her a few weeks or at a pinch, months, then she'll be back to normal'. But we never get back to 'normal', we never get over it because to get over it would mean we were not changed by our devastating loss.

The death of our child changes us. Gradually, very gradually, with the help of understanding friends, especially those in TCF, who are on the same journey, we survive and start to grow within ourselves, to begin to offer comfort and support to other bereaved parents, to begin to make a difference to their lives and to ours. Life is not the same as before but we begin to live again, to enjoy the coming and going of the seasons, to remember our children and carry them with us, a precious part of us, in whatever we do. And we learn to smile again:

Illusion?
Did I really smile just then?
        Or was it just the usual pretence?
And the rose I noticed over there -
        How did I see it as rich red?
But... I heard a bird sing yesterday,

And listened to the song,
And I recognised that special menu
By odours wafting through the air.

Hello, you senses, long forgotten
When grief strode in and claimed our lives.
Goodbye, pretence, it's really happening...
Real smiles and sights and sounds and touch,
Like blinded seeing for the first time,
Or paralysed begin to walk,
The faltering steps - the past accepted
The signs I'm learning to live again.
Audrey England, *from 'Helping Ourselves'*

I love the following story, *Kafka and the Doll.* Many a truth about life can be revealed in a simple tale.

KAFKA AND THE DOLL, *The Pervasiveness of Loss*

Franz Kafka, the story goes, encountered a little girl in the park where he went walking daily. She was crying. *She had lost her doll and was desolate. Kafka offered to help her look for the doll and arranged to meet her the next day at the same spot.*

Unable to find the doll, he composed a letter from the doll and read it to her when they met. 'Please do not mourn me, I have gone on a trip to see the world. I will write you of my adventures.'

This was the beginning of many letters. When he and the little girl met he read to her from these carefully composed letters the imagined adventures of the beloved doll. The little girl was comforted.

When the meetings came to an end Kafka presented her with a doll. She obviously looked different from the original doll. An attached letter explained, 'My travels have changed me.'

Many years later, the now grown girl found a letter stuffed into an unnoticed crevice in the cherished replacement doll. In summary it said:

'Every thing that you love, you will eventually lose, but in the end, love will return in a different form.'

After a While
After a while you learn the subtle difference
Between holding a hand and chaining a soul,
And you learn that love doesn't mean leaning
and company doesn't mean security.

And you begin to learn that kisses aren't contracts
And presents aren't promises,
And you begin to accept your defeats
With your head up and your eyes open
With the grace of a woman, not the grief of a child.

And you learn to build all your roads
On today because tomorrow's ground
Is too uncertain for plans, and futures have
A way of falling down in mid-flight.

After a while you learn that even sunshine
Burns if you get too much.

So you plant your own garden and decorate
Your own soul, instead of waiting
For someone to bring you flowers.

And you learn that you really can endure…
That you really are strong
And you really do have worth.

And you learn and learn…
With every goodbye you learn.

Veronica A Shoffstall

***

'Grief does not change you... It reveals you.' John
Green

***

Bricks

For every tear you hold back
Another brick appears in the wall in front of you.
For every minute you hold back
The mortar sets.

Allow the tears to flow…
for they alone can dissolve the mortar.
As the tears cascade freely down your face
The mortar softens
The brick wall wavers.

One by one,
Tear by tear,
The bricks topple.
They hit the ground
Shatter into tiny pieces.

Step over them and take a tiny step forward.
Every journey starts with a step forward.

Many brick walls will appear before you on your journey.
Never fret about the 'last' one, there won't be a last one;
For now, deal with the one in front of you
You know how to do it now…

Cazz Fleet

Yes, many brick walls did appear before me on my grief journey and at times I felt like giving up completely. I didn't want to go on. I lost all interest in life, I lost all interest in myself as a person. I wasn't me any more.

Looking back now, I acknowledge the hard graft it was to gain any kind of interest in living and to become 'me' again - not the same me as before but a 'me' that has survived and grown. Now I can think of the saying by Oscar Wilde and smile:

'Be yourself; everyone else is already taken.'

You will survive this journey of grief too; you will change and you will grow. You will carry your children with you; your love for them and their love for you will sustain and support you; it will help to give you the strength and commitment you need to face each new day, to face it with hope and with courage and eventually to reach out and support others, and to make a difference. To put it simply:

'Don't just *be* yourself, *become* yourself.'

Dear friends, we have been on a journey together; I leave you now with part of the Compassionate Friends Creed:

'We are all seeking and struggling to build a future for ourselves, but we are committed to building that future together as we reach out to each other in love, and share the pain as well as the joy, share the anger as well as the peace, share the faith as well as the doubts and help each other to grieve as well as to grow.'

READING SUGGESTIONS

Compiled by our TCF Librarian, Mary Hartley

Books for Everyone

Aspects of Loss by Gill Hartley

Bereaved Parents and their Continuing Bonds by Catherine Seigal

Knowing Why Changes Nothing by Eva Lager with Sasha Wagner (A mixture of prose and poetry by two mums who lost children; Eva's daughter died from suicide)

Always With You by Gloria Hunniford

A Heartbeat Away: finding Hope following grief and loss by Flappy Lane Fox

For the Love of Mike by Anne Hilary Phillips

A Manual for Heartache by Cathy Rentzenbrink

Beyond Tears: living after losing a child by Ellen Mitchell

Holding onto Love: searching for hope when a child dies by Chuck Collins

Dear Parents by Joy Johnson

Bearing the Unbearable: love, loss, and the heartbreaking path of grief by Joanne Cacciatore

It's OK that you're NOT OK: meeting grief and loss in a culture that doesn't understand by Megan Devine

Books to Help after a Suicide

Suicide Survivors: a guide for those left behind by Adina Wrobleski

Suicide: Why?: 85 questions and answers about suicide by Adina Wrobleski

Suicide of a Child: by Adina Wrobleski (whose daughter died from suicide)

Losing a Child: explorations in grief by Linda Hurcombe (Linda's daughter died from suicide but this book is helpful for all parents; it's full of good advice)

My Son, My Son: a guide to healing after a suicide in the family by Iris Bolton with Corin Michell

Searching for my Estrella Maili: rebuilding my life after the death of my daughter by Gisela Castillo de Lujan

Do They Have Bad Days in Heaven?: surviving the suicide loss of a sibling by Michelle Linn-Gust.

His Bright Light: The Story of My Son, Nick Traina by Danielle Steel (a book about the author's son who suffered from bi-polar disease and died from suicide)

No Time To Say Goodbye by Carla Fine

Books to Help after a Death from Suicide or Substance Use

See You Soon by Philippa Skinner

Junkie Buddha: : A Journey of Discovery in Peru by Diane Esguerra

Ben: Diary of a Heroin Addict by Anne Rogers

lukelove: My Boy, My Grief, My Journal by Sheila Scott

Mum Can You Lend Me Twenty Quid? by Elizabeth Burton-Phillips

Books for Siblings

Surviving a Sibling: discovering life after loss by Scott Mastley

Letters to Sara: the agony of adult sibling loss by Anne McCurry

The Last Act of Love: the story of my brother and his sister by Cathy Rentzenbrink

The Day That Went Missing by Richard Beard

The Web of Grief by Rhiannon Jones

From a Clear Blue Sky: surviving the Mountbatten bomb by Timothy Knatchbull (whose twin brother, Nicky, died)

Books for Children

I Miss my Sister by Sarah Courtauld and Holly Surplice

The Sad Book by Michael Rosen

Water Bugs and Dragonflies by Doris Stickney

Let's Talk About When Someone Dies by Molly Potter

Books for Grandparents

When a Grandchild Dies: what to do, what to say, how to cope, by Nadine Galinsky

Grandparents Cry Twice: help for bereaved grandparents

by Mary Lou Reed

Books to Help after a Murder

A Song for Jenny: a mother's story of love and loss by Julie Nicholson (whose daughter died in the 7/7 London bombings)

For the Love of Julie by Ann Ming

An Ordinary Murder by Lesley Moorhead

Tim, an Ordinary Boy by Colin and Wendy Parry

Goodbye Dearest Holly by Kevin Wells (Although the Soham murders were horrific, Holly's dad is basically a positive person and I came away from this book with the feeling that his family had been neither defeated nor destroyed by the man who'd taken their daughter and sister from them)

Books of Hope

When Bad Things Happen to Good People by Harold S Kushner (This author is a rabbi whose son died at the age of 14 from the premature ageing disease. He uses his knowledge of theology to try to understand why God would do such a thing to him)

On Life after Death by Elizabeth Kubler-Ross, a doctor whose work with sick and dying children made her certain that life continues after physical death

The Truth in the Light: an investigation of over 300 near death experiences by Peter Fenwick and Elizabeth Fenwick

Life after Life by Raymond Moody who has written

a number of books on the subject of near death experiences

Candles on the Ganges by Peter Upton

Poetry

Don't Let Them Tell You How to Grieve: everyday jottings that tell it exactly how it is by Gina Claye (Going to the solicitor's but the car takes you to Tescos, being forgetful and putting salt in your tea, reminding yourself to 'put one foot in front of the other and don't forget to breathe…')

The Swallow, the Owl and the Sandpiper: words of courage, wisdom and spirit compiled by Claire Maitland

Broken Heart still Beats: a compilation of poetry and prose by Anne McCracken and Mary Semel

Books for Fathers (and for Mothers too)

Kadian Journal: a father's journal following the sudden death of his young son, by Thomas Harding

Against the Dying of the Light: a father's journey through grief, by Leonard Fein

One for Sorrow by Alan Hargrave

Dear Charlie: letters to a lost daughter, by Reg Thompson

Losing a Child and the Grieving Experience by Bruce Watt

Fiction

The Knitting Circle by Ann Hood

Over by Margaret Forster

Drift by Jenny Alexander

The Accidental Tourist by Anne Tyler

THE COMPASSIONATE FRIENDS

The Compassionate Friends is a national and international organisation of bereaved parents, siblings and grandparents offering support, understanding and friendship to others after the loss of a child, of any age, from any cause.

Our national Helpline is staffed by volunteers who are bereaved parents themselves and offers support and information 365 days a year.

We also offer:
- a comprehensive website and moderated online community forum
- local support groups and one-to-one support
- weekend gatherings and retreats
- group support via social media in private, well-moderated Facebook groups
- information leaflets, bereavement support publications and a unique postal library on all aspects of bereavement
- some specialist support for adult bereaved siblings is also available.

Please contact us to find out more.
Helpline: 0345 123 2304
Hours: daily from 10.00-16.00 and 19.00-22.00

Northern Ireland Helpline: 0288 77 88 016
Open every day of the year from 10:00 – 16:00 and 19:00 – 21:30

Website: www.tcf.org.uk

Support pages on the website: www.tcf.org.uk/support

Email: helpline@tcf.org.uk

Follow us on Facebook at https://www.facebook.com/www.tcf.org.uk/

Twitter @TCFcharityUK

THE COMPASSIONATE FRIENDS CREED

We need not walk alone.

We are The Compassionate Friends.

We reach out to each other with love, with understanding and with hope.

Our children have died at all ages and from many different causes, but our love for our children unites us.

Your pain becomes my pain, just as your hope becomes my hope.

We come together from all walks of life, from many different circumstances.

We are a unique family because we represent many races and creeds.

We are young and we are old.

Some of us are far along in our grief, but others still feel a grief so fresh and so intensely painful that we feel hopeless and see no hope.

Some of us have found faith to be a source of strength; some of us are struggling to find answers.

Some of us are angry, filled with guilt or in deep depression; others radiate an inner peace.

But whatever pain we bring to this gathering of The Compassionate Friends, it is pain we will share, just as we share with each other our love for our children.

We are all seeking and struggling to build a future for ourselves, but we are committed to building that future together as we reach out to each other in love and share the pain as well as the joy, share the anger as well as the peace, share the faith as well as the doubts and help each other to grieve as well as to grow.

DON'T LET THEM TELL YOU HOW TO GRIEVE

ISBN 978-1-910779-11-8

ISBN Kindle edition 978-1-78018-519-4

ISBN EPub edition 978-1-78018-520-0

Gina Claye's poems tell it exactly as it is after one has suffered a traumatic bereavement: the intense grief, overwhelming emotions, thinking you're going mad, feeling totally exhausted, being absentminded so you put salt instead of sugar in your much needed cup of tea.

They describe the inability to cope with daily activities, feeling that you belong to a different world from everyone else, wondering if you'll ever find meaning in your life again and being so forgetful that the car ends up in Tescos when you meant to drive to the solicitors. Above all, these lines let you know that you're not alone.

Lightning Source UK Ltd.
Milton Keynes UK
UKHW012005261021
392884UK00001B/40